Pregnant

With Christ

A Vision of the Expectant Church

---

by

Phillip L. Carter

and

Vivian Q. Carter

Published by Serenity Books

ISBN 1-58158-028-2

Printed in the United States of America
For Worldwide Distribution

Dedication

To our parents, Logan and Sara Carter, and Al Quinter and Charlene Quinter Keever.

To our children, Phil and Jenny, and our grandchildren, Andee, Joshua, T.J. and Zachary.

To pastors everywhere, whose greatest rewards will be received in Heaven.

Acknowledgments

Special thanks to Harold McDougal for his invaluable help with this manuscript. Also thanks to Bishop Houston Miles, Pastor Burt McDaniel, Evangelist Buddy Barron, Wayne Bowen, CPA, and Dody Griffith for their time in reading the manuscript, as well as their helpful suggestions.

Contents

Introduction

This book is a prophetic assessment of the state of the Church of our Lord Jesus Christ today, and regardless of your eschatology, after you read it, you must come to an undeniable conclusion: We who have been born again are all *Pregnant With Christ*! Even the most casual Christian observer cannot help but see the signs of the times all around us. The imminent return of our Lord is being addressed through books, magazines, the pulpit, television — both religious and secular — radio, and even the Internet. Many are receiving revelation of things kept secret since the foundation of the world. We are on the verge of something very important.

Jesus gave me the revelation for this book in my daily quiet time. At first I thought it was to be a sermon, but He made it clear that the message was to be much more widely dispersed. We are indeed *Pregnant With Christ*, and it is now the ninth month. As you read through the book, picture yourself carrying the Christ Child within — even as Mary did. The conception of the Church took place on the Day of Pentecost, but our personal conceptions occurred when we were born again.

There is, however, an abortionist — Satan — who is intent on destroying the life within us. In the coming pages, we will examine the plan of our common enemy to harm us in this way. We will follow his schemes to destroy life from the beginning of time.

Soon our pregnancy will become apparent to everyone. Even the world will recognize the sons of God in their ninth month of pregnancy. As an expectant woman cannot hide the Child within, neither can we pregnant ones hide the child we are carrying. In the coming days, we will experience stretch marks along with other discomforts of pregnancy. Childbirth classes will prepare us for these discomforts, as they also prepare us for the birth.

In these pages, we will learn to recognize the signs of the end times. We will see the labor pains as the final groanings of the Church to bring forth this Child. Understanding the signs will help us feel prepared for the task ahead.

We will see that we have a Great Physician taking care of us. We can trust Him to make the right decisions for us. His interest is in the health of this Child. He will do everything within His power to bring forth a strong and healthy Child.

We will learn how much the Husband is expectantly waiting for this Child. His faithfulness to us, the pregnant ones, is evident to all. The Husband will comfort, strengthen and encourage us, and He will be present during the birth of the Child. The birth is what it is all about.

Finally, we will come to the long-awaited birth. As all creation recognizes the sons of God upon earth, the abortionist (Satan) will realize that his plans have failed. The pregnant ones have been prepared through the childbirth classes. When labor pains begin, the pregnant ones anticipate the final outcome. The Physician (God the Father) has cared for the pregnant ones well. He is assured the Child will come forth in health. As the last pains begin, the expectant Husband (Jesus) stands tall. The long-awaited event is about to take place. As the Child comes forth, the Physician cuts the umbilical cord and the birth (the Rapture) takes place. With a loud cry, the child comes forth. The Husband reaches forth His strong arms and receives the Child in midair as the angels in Heaven rejoice!

For we know that the whole creation groans and suffers the pains of childbirth together until now.
Romans 8:22

Chapter 1

The Setting

And Mary said to the angel, "How can this be, since I am a virgin?"
And the angel answered and said to her, "The Holy Spirit will come upon you, and the power of the Most High will overshadow you; and for that reason the holy offspring shall be called the Son of God."   Luke 1:34-35

One day, as I was reading this passage in Luke's gospel, the Holy Spirit spoke to me about the birthing process through which Christ came into the world as a man. The Spirit did not give me the complete revelation in that moment, but I sensed that He had something special to share with me. This He did over a period of several months (and He continues to show me more). It occurred to me that *"the power of the Most High"* has overshadowed us, much as it did Mary, and that *"the holy offspring"* being birthed in us is also called *"the Son of God."* In that moment, I realized for the first time that we, as believers, are *Pregnant With Christ*.

We Are Pregnant!

Paul spoke of this matter OF CHRIST IN US when he wrote, *"To whom God willed to make known what is the riches of the glory of this mystery among the Gentiles, which is CHRIST IN YOU, the hope of glory"* (Colossians 1:27). This *"CHRIST IN YOU"* is the same Christ that the Virgin Mary was pregnant with two thousand years ago. Now, YOU are pregnant with Christ. He is in you.

When writing to the Romans, Paul spoke more definitely of Christ being revealed when he said, *"For the anxious longing of the creation waits eagerly for the revealing of the sons of God"* (Romans 8:19).

In Jesus' time, there was an old man named Simeon whom God had promised that he would not die until he saw the Christ of God, until He was revealed to him, until he held Him in his arms. We believers need the determination of Simeon as we wait expectantly for our revealing of Christ once again. Christ is coming again, and before He does, the world will know that the sons of God are walking on earth.

Jesus is longing for His perfect Bride, and His Bride, the Church, is being perfected and impregnated with His love and power. Now, those pregnant ones who are expectantly looking for Him are very soon to give birth.

As the Child within us is birthed, we will meet the Lord in the air. We are now in the third trimester; we are in the ninth month; we are on the way to the hospital right now. We have received the greatest responsibility of any generation of Christians that has ever lived, and it is time that we become aware of our responsibility and

of the day and hour in which we live. The mystery of
godliness and the sons of God are about to be revealed.
We are entering the time of the greatest anointing and
the greatest warfare the world has ever known.

As we read the account of the glory of the birth of
Christ in a manger, how much more shall the glory of
Christ be upon the sons of God when He is revealed at
His second coming!

The gospel of Luke tells of His birth:

> *And she gave birth to her firstborn son; and she*
> *wrapped Him in cloths, and laid him in a manger,*
> *because there was no room for them in the inn.*
> *And in the same region there were some shepherds*
> *staying out in the fields, and keeping watch over*
> *their flock by night. And an angel of the Lord sud-*
> *denly stood before them, and the glory of the Lord*
> *shown round about them; and they were terribly*
> *frightened. And the angel said to them, "Do not be*
> *afraid; for behold, I bring you good news of a great*
> *joy which shall be for all the people; for today in the*
> *city of David there has been born for you a Savior,*
> *who is Christ the Lord. And this will be a sign for*
> *you: you will find a baby wrapped in cloths, and*
> *lying in a manger." And suddenly there appeared*
> *with the angel a multitude of the heavenly host*
> *praising God, and saying,*
> *"Glory to God in the highest,*
> *And on earth peace among men with whom He is*
> *pleased."*   Luke 2:7-14

Other generations of Christians — including Paul, Peter, James and John — are in Heaven right now, wishing that they could have lived today. They experienced God's love, power and glory at Jesus' first appearing, but they know that His second appearing will be far greater in every dimension of God's glory and power. Jesus is now speaking to His apostles and prophets to declare, "The hour is at hand; wake up and arise and enter into the destiny I have prepared for My last-hour Church."

We have the tremendous privilege and responsibility of living in this hour and being the generation that will usher in Christ's return. Hebrews speaks of this:

> *Therefore, since we have so great a CLOUD OF WITNESSES surrounding us, let us also lay aside every encumbrance, and the sin which so easily entangles us, and let us run with endurance the race that is set before us.* Hebrews 12:1

The race has begun. The baton has been handed off for the last time lap. We must now cross the finish line with it. The Holy Spirit is helping us run faster, as the pace is quickening. This holy wind has begun to blow and will continue with increasing velocity as the appointed time comes.

For some years now, revival winds have been blowing strongly in Argentina, Brazil, Nigeria, South Korea and many other countries of the world. Now pockets of this supernatural wind of revival are breaking out in the United States and Canada. This is an indication of the urgency of the time in which we are living.

Argentina

What has come to be called "The Renewal" in Argentina has been nothing short of remarkable. Most agree that the evangelist Carlos Annacondia has been God's primary chosen vessel of this generation for that nation. Although many other dedicated men and women of God are being used in Argentina, Carlos Annacondia seems to be God's chosen apostle for this generation. As he preaches to tens of thousands of expectant, needy people, not only are thousands saved and baptized with the Holy Spirit, but many are supernaturally healed by the power of God. Many people fall under the power of God in his meetings and have manifestations similar to those we read about in the gospels. Demons come out of those who are possessed.

Carlos Annacondia has written about some of these revival meetings and the personal testimonies of those whose lives have been radically changed by the power of God in his book *Listen to Me, Satan.* There, he also gives his account of receiving the baptism of the Holy Spirit: "The night I received the baptism of the Holy Spirit marked myself and my ministry forever. It was during a meeting with Evangelist Manuel Ruiz. We started to pray and worship God. In a few minutes most of the people in the place were speaking in new tongues. Maria, my wife, looked like an angel. She was singing and speaking in tongues with such fluency.

"I suddenly realized that everybody was receiving the baptism except me. From the depth of my soul, I wanted to receive the baptism they were receiving. I started to cry out to God with all my heart, 'Lord, baptize me or I will die!' I had only known Him for a week, and I was already experiencing incredible things.

"As I was crying out to God with all that was within me, asking for His baptism, lightning fell over me from Heaven. It was God's power. It threw me to the ground, and I started to speak in new tongues. I was speaking one language after another, all throughout that night. By the next day I had lost my voice, and it has never been the same since.

"The Lord gave me a vision that night. I saw myself in a large stadium, three stories high, speaking to one hundred and fifty thousand people." [1]

Before long, Carlos Annacondia was preaching to thousands and then to millions of people in Argentina. He is now in demand all over the world, including the United States.

Brazil

Brazil was one example of the amazing growth of the Pentecostal/Charismatic Body of Christ in South America in the twentieth century. In 1900, there were less than a hundred thousand evangelical Christians in Brazil. By 1990, however, there were already twenty-six million evangelical believers, nearly eighteen percent of the entire population of the country. [2]

Recently, I had lunch with a friend who has ministered throughout South America for years. He says that Brazil needs tens of thousands of pastors and that many of the pastors there are over several churches and they often work full-time secular jobs as well. They are, therefore, in a continual state of exhaustion in their labor for our Lord. The harvest is truly ripe in Brazil as never before.

Nigeria

In Lagos, Nigeria, God raised up the largest Christian church in Africa — William Kumuyi's Deeper Life Bible Church — which, by 1995, was drawing over two hundred thousand worshippers each week. [3]

South Korea

Surprisingly, many modern American Christians are not very well informed about the revival that has been taking place in South Korea over the past twenty years. I was blessed to attend a pastors' conference many years ago at which one of the speakers was a small Korean named Dr. David Yonggi Cho. At that time, his church was already very large — nearly ten thousand members — but he said that God had given him a vision for fifty thousand. Apparently, God later gave him several other visions, because today he pastors seven hundred and fifty thousand people.

In his book *Prayer That Brings Revival*, Dr. Cho said: "Yoido Full Gospel Church, the church I pastor in Seoul, Korea, with its seven hundred and fifty thousand members, is the world's largest church. Every month, as many as seven hundred new converts are being saved from Buddhism, secularism and nominal Christian backgrounds. How can a church grow this large? Is it possible for other countries to have this kind of revival? I am convinced that renewal is possible anywhere people dedicate themselves to prayer.

"When I began my pastoral ministry in 1958, I went to Dae Jo Dong, a poor area outside of Seoul. I pitched a U.S. Army tent and began to preach. I remember so well actually living in my tent, spending my nights in prayer. During our cold Korean winters, I would cover myself with blankets and, lying near my pulpit, would spend many long hours in prayer. Soon, other members of my small congregation began to join with me in prayer. In a short period of time, more than fifty people were gathering to spend entire nights in prayer. This is how I began my ministry.

"People come to my office for prayer regularly. I have seen the lame walk, the blind see and the paralyzed leap from their wheelchairs by the power of God. Am I special? God has no special children. We can all have power in prayer — if we are willing to pay the price." [4]

Canada

On January 20, 1994, a significant revival broke out at Pastor John Arnott's Toronto Airport Church in Toronto, Canada. By the end of 1997, nearly two million visitors had come there from nearly every nation under Heaven to be blessed by the flow of it. [5]

The United States

As Vivian and I have been traveling and speaking, attending various pastors' conferences, and talking to others who have also been traveling and speaking in various churches throughout this country, we all see the same thing. There is the beginning of a powerful move of God's Spirit in select places. I intended to list some of these places (other than Brownsville Assembly of God in Pensacola, Florida, with which everyone seems to be familiar), but God's Spirit has broken out in so many churches throughout the country recently that it became impossible for me to choose which ones to list. At this writing, there are literally hundreds of churches throughout our nation that are experiencing similar outpourings of the Holy Spirit.

Despite the sprinklings of rain that we are feeling, there is a great spiritual need here in America. The United States has not experienced a major revival in more than a hundred years, and not one of the fifty largest churches in the world is to be found here on our soil. Those of us who are *Pregnant With Christ* must cry out to God as never before that He will send revival to more and more parts of America before it is eternally too late. The hour is very, very late, and judgment on this nation will not be delayed much longer. We need a major revival of repentance. We have church buildings on every street corner, and yet God looks at us as He did on the people of Isaiah's day:

> *"Bring your worthless offerings no longer,*
> *Incense is an abomination to Me.*
> *New moon and sabbath, the calling of assemblies —*
> *I cannot endure iniquity and the solemn assembly.*
> *I hate your new moon festivals and your appointed feasts,*

They have become a burden to Me.
I am weary of bearing them.
So when you spread out your hands in prayer,
I will hide My eyes from you,
Yes, even though you multiply prayers,
I will not listen.
Your hands are covered with blood.
Wash yourselves, make yourselves clean;
Remove the evil of your deeds from My sight.
Cease to do evil,
Learn to do good;
Seek justice,
Reprove the ruthless;
Defend the orphan,
Plead for the widow."   Isaiah 1:13-17

As in Isaiah's day, most of the church services held in America are now no more than ceremonial gatherings. Not only do most of America's preachers have no power in their services, they do not even believe God is capable of bringing His power to His people.

David Wilkerson speaks of America's need of repentance in his book *America's Last Call:* "America's present prosperity is God's last mercy call before His chastening occurs! Consider the days of Noah — prosperity was the last call! Consider the days of Lot — prosperity was the last call! Consider the days of King Josiah — prosperity was the last call! Consider the fall of Babylon — prosperity was the last call! One of the most convincing evidences of all is found in Jeremiah 44. Overnight, Judah's good days turned into a hellish nightmare. Overpowering armies flooded Jerusalem, burning the temple and reducing the city to rubble. The remnant of Israel had to flee for their lives to Egypt. Yet, even after all this calamity, the remnant continued their idolatry, sacrificing to false gods." [6]

Idolatry is again rampant on the earth. Even so, God's mercy is extended to those who are hungering and thirsting after Him.

Who Will Participate?

Not all Evangelical or even Charismatic/Pentecostal churches will experience the coming outpouring of God's Spirit. Frank Bartleman's comments concerning the Azusa Street Revival apply today: "Some churches are going to be surprised to find God passing them by. He will work in channels where they will yield to Him. They must humble themselves for Him to come. We are crying, 'Pasadena for God!' but some people are too satisfied with their own goodness. They have little faith or interest for the salvation of others. God will humble them by passing them by. The Spirit is breathing prayer for us for a mighty, general outpouring. We are praying for the churches and their pastors. The Lord will visit those willing to yield to Him." [7]

We Will See Change

We who have this wonderful privilege of being *Pregnant With Christ* in this day and hour should rejoice as we greet one another, even as Elizabeth rejoiced when

she greeted the mother of her Lord. Luke records this
wonderful event:

> *Now at this time Mary arose and went with haste to*
> *the hill country, to a city of Judah, and entered the*
> *house of Zacharias and greeted Elizabeth. And it*
> *came about that when Elizabeth heard Mary's greet-*
> *ing, the baby leaped in her womb: and Elizabeth was*
> *filled with the Holy Spirit. And she cried out with a*
> *loud voice, and said, "Blessed among women are you,*
> *and blessed is the fruit of your womb! And how has*
> *it happened to me, that the mother of my Lord should*
> *come to me? For behold, when the sound of your*
> *greeting reached my ears, the baby leaped in my*
> *womb for joy."*   Luke 1:39-44

Soon, as we greet one another, the Christ Child whom
we carry will also leap within us. Soon, all divisions,
gossiping, backbiting, power struggles and many other
such things that have held us apart will disappear among
the pregnant ones, for we will be united with one mind
and purpose. We, like Elizabeth, will greet one another
with great humility, knowing that from the least to the
greatest, we are each in the process of birthing our Lord.
We will no longer be wise in our own estimation, and
no longer will we merely look out for our own personal
interests. With an unselfishness and love that has rarely
occurred in the history of the Church, we will help one
another in this birthing process.

Can you imagine how Mary felt when she realized she
was pregnant with the Messiah, the Savior of the world,

the King of the universe? How many times would she ask the question, "Why me?"?

Somehow, I believe Mary came to terms with her destiny quickly. How precious was the seed she carried! Mary was very conscientious of the One within her, taking care to nourish, protect, guard and defend Him whom she carried.

She would have laid down her life for the babe within. She wanted to make sure that the stresses of life did not rob her of bringing forth this Christ, full term and in health. I believe Mary did everything she could to ensure that the child would be born.

We Must Make Preparation

Can you imagine the anticipation Mary experienced as she looked forward to that day? You should be able to imagine it, because, my friend, you also are carrying the Christ Child. As believers, we are to be just as careful to care for the Christ within us as Mary was with her pregnancy. We need to make sure our nourishment comes from feeding upon the Word of God, so that the Christ within us will grow to maturity. We need to protect the Christ within us by making right choices, surrounding ourselves with other believers for support, and shunning the ways of the world. We need to guard the Christ within us, by boldly confessing Him when challenged. And we need to defend His name and His Word, even if it should mean giving our lives.

When we grab hold of the revelation that we are indeed as *Pregnant With Christ* as Mary was, how full our joy will be! We are growing and stretching! We are laboring toward the goal! We are anticipating the long-awaited birth!

The intensity of the worship of our Lord in this ninth month will be greater than when Solomon's Temple was dedicated.

> *And it came about when the priests came from the holy place, that the cloud filled the house of the LORD, so that the priests could not stand to minister because of the cloud, for the glory of the LORD filled the house of the Lord.*
> *Then Solomon said,*
> *"The LORD has said that He would dwell in the thick cloud.*
> *I have surely built Thee a lofty house, a place for Thy dwelling forever."*   1 Kings 8:10-13

We are that lofty house now, and we are that dwelling place for the Christ who is about to be birthed. The worship that is about to proceed forth from us will be so powerful, and the manifestation of God's presence will be so real, that the glory displayed in Solomon's day will seem to be a mere shadow of what is displayed in our ninth month of pregnancy.

During the Azusa Street Revival, at the turn of the century, this type of worship was experienced for a brief period of time. There was much singing in the Spirit that could only be described as angelic, as God's people totally yielded themselves to the true worship that God so desires. For, He said, the true believers worship in Spirit and truth.

The songs that will be written in the days to come will be composed with great longing for this Child to be born, because they will spring forth from the Child who is in us. They will express great gratitude and will describe the power and majesty that will soon occur at this birth. Many songs currently being given by the Spirit typify this ninth month pregnancy and the renewal movement that accompanies it. For instance, the Holy Spirit is giving songs to the Church describing the Christ as a great Warrior, because He will fight the great battle of the end time for us. The Church, in this last hour, will take on the personality of a conquering warrior because she is pregnant with her Conquering Warrior. Therefore, the Holy Spirit will give many victorious warrior songs to the Church. This worship will tear down strongholds that have never before been defeated by the Church. This worship will enable the Church to usher in a conquering hero, not a defeated foe.

Pregnant ones, lift up your heads, for your redemption draweth nigh, and you will give birth, departing from here in victory. We will have the great honor of fighting this last great battle because He is in us. He will be birthed as the Overcoming Warrior.

Endnotes

1. *Listen to Me, Satan,* Carlos Annacondia, Creation House, Orlando, FL, 1998, p. 112.
2. *Floods Upon the Dry Ground,* Charles P. Schmitt, Destiny Image Publishers, Shippensburg, PA, 1998, Chapter 12, p. 233.
3. Ibid, p. 233.
4. *Prayer That Brings Revival,* Dr. David Yonggi Cho, Creation House, Orlando, FL, 1998, Introduction, p. xi.

5. *Floods Upon the Dry Ground*, Charles P. Schmitt, Destiny
   Image Publishers, Shippensburg, PA, 1998, Chapter 12, pp.
   233, 236.
6. *America's Last Call*, David Wilkerson, Wilkerson Trust
   Publications, Lindale, TX, 1998, pp. 12-16.
7. *Azusa Street*, Frank Bartleman, Whitaker House, 1982, p. 9.

Chapter 2

The Conception

*For all who are being led by the Spirit of God, these
are sons of God. For you have not received a spirit
of slavery leading to fear again, but you have received a spirit of adoption as sons by which we cry
out, "Abba! Father!" The Spirit Himself bears witness with our spirit that we are children of God.*
Romans 8:14-16

In 1976, I was a junior partner in a small CPA firm in
north Georgia. God allowed circumstances in my life that
caused me to develop a great hunger to know Him and
experience Him, even though I had no idea what that
really meant. After reading the Bible through and going
down many different roads (that only seemed to lead to
a similar dead end), my dental hygienist gave me two
books that changed my life forever.

One of the books was the autobiography of Pat
Robertson, *Shout It From the Housetops,* and the other was
The Cross and the Switchblade by David Wilkerson. I read
about Pat Robertson's journey of faith and his search for
the baptism of the Holy Spirit, and I read about how
David had gone to the ghettos of New York City, where

God had used him to set gang members free through the power of the Spirit. As I read, I somehow knew that the experience these two men were describing was real. I could not doubt its validity, and I wanted it.

What we read in those books, in fact, created a great hunger in both of us, and not long afterward, we received this wonderful experience from God. Vivian remembers ...

In 1974, I found myself at a very empty place in my life. The detail of how I got there must be reserved for another book. Suffice it to say that I was disillusioned with just about everything and everyone that I had once counted dear to me, and I had begun to search for something more meaningful in life. Having been a stay-at-home mom for many years, I decided that the thing I needed was to establish an identity of my own. I decided to find a job and began working at a local hospital as a secretary. A short time later, I was invited to a Bible study attended by some of my co-workers. I was totally unaware of the fact that my life was about to take a radical turn.

Our little group was led by a lady who was a product of the sixties, and who had been converted on the streets of downtown Atlanta. It was during the Hippie Movement, and they hung out on 10th Street downtown. This lady was from a wealthy family, but she chose to live on the streets with the other hippies and "do her own thing." She was into the drug-and-free-sex culture. What made her so unusual was that she left behind a fine husband and several children to go through this "second childhood."

Then one day someone had given her a salvation tract

with the "Roman Road" on it, and she had been gloriously saved. Now, many years later, she found herself teaching women how to be born again, and I found myself in one of her studies.

Having gone to traditional churches most of my life, I had never heard the simple plan of salvation, and upon hearing it, I knew that this was the key to happiness I had been looking for.

Digging Deeper

Even though it was a shallow walk at first, I began the best way I knew to live for the Lord. It wasn't until a year later, when I began to search for a deeper walk, that I really began to grow. At that time, Phillip and I were both searching for the baptism in the Holy Spirit. We had read some books on the experience and immediately decided it was for us. The problem we had was in knowing someone, a real, live person, to ask about it. Everyone we knew was filled with the spirit all right, but not the Holy Spirit.

I thought of our next-door neighbors. Everyone talked about them as being very religious and a little strange, but they had always been very sweet and friendly to us. I decided to overcome my fear and call on the lady of the house.

I knocked on her door one day and said to her, "I want you to tell me about the Lord." She almost shouted, and gladly welcomed me in. For the next few hours, we talked about the Holy Spirit. It was so wonderful to be around someone who really knew about this matter.

Before I left that day, my neighbor asked me if I would like to go to a Bible study at her pastor's home one night later that week. I told her I would ask my husband. Thus began our introduction to the Holy Spirit.

Try to get a mental picture of this. I was a very quiet, dependent, in-the-background person, and Phillip had always made me feel that he was much more spiritual than I was. I had no knowledge of the Bible whatsoever, but I also did not have any of the preconceived expectations common to many denominations. Actually, I was a very good candidate for God's power.

Couple this with the childlike faith that God had given to me (it was nothing that I could boast about), and you *really* had a good candidate. The only thing I was up against was fear, and that night at the home of my neighbor's pastor, I was feeling all that I could take.

As we approached his house that night, he opened the door to us. When I looked at him, all I saw was eyes. I had seen eyes before, but this man's eyes seemed to be looking directly into my soul. Although I could not have realized it that night, I would see many more eyes like this man's over the years, but this was a first.

These were the eyes of a man under the anointing of God. I felt like he knew everything I was thinking and everything about my past. The truth of the matter was that he did know something. Our neighbor had alerted the group that we were coming, and they had been praying for hours already — just for us.

As we listened to the teaching that night on the Holy Spirit (tailored just for us), the hunger in me grew. I was still afraid of the crowd, and unwilling to speak up (that

was my nature in any crowd, for my life was one of in-
security), but when the pastor concluded his teaching
and asked for anyone who wanted to be filled to come
forward, I was strangely moved. Phillip went forward
and prayed, but he did not immediately receive. Then
"the eyes" focused on me in the crowd, and the next
thing I knew I was surrounded by people who were lay-
ing hands on me and raising their voices in prayer for
me.

This was a terrifying experience. Part of me really
wanted everything the Lord had, and that was why we
had come there, but another part could not concentrate
on the task at hand for the activity going on around me.

I felt my whole body go numb, and my lips began to
quiver so violently that I could not control them. Still, I
was too timid to speak out in other tongues.

I had read enough in books to know what I should be
doing. I knew how to yield to the Holy Spirit, but I was
too timid to do it in front of these people. Sensing the
problem, the pastor instructed me to go home and do it
in the privacy of my bedroom. That night, on the way
home, everyone laughed at me because I couldn't talk.
My tongue and lips were quivering and numb, and I
couldn't say anything.

A Divine Visitation

Quietly, in my bed that night, I prayed to the Lord
that He would fill me and forgive me for being so fearful. I had always had a sense that the Lord understood
my nature and did not condemn me for it. He had al-

ways been good to let me grow at a pace I could handle. I drifted off into a peaceful sleep that evening, hoping God would answer my prayer.

Sometime during the night (I'm not sure of the time), I was awakened. Phillip was asleep by my side, but it was as though I was alone in the bed. I was not, however, alone in the room. I sensed a presence in the room like nothing I ever felt — before or since.

I could not open my eyes; I could not move; I could not speak. I lay in the bed in that state for an undefined moment of time. More than twenty years later, I can still remember clearly the feeling of that moment. I felt a love I could not describe, and a peace that passes understanding.

After a time, I was able to open my eyes. I was not prepared for what I saw. I was still frozen in time and could not move any other part of my body. For all practical purposes, Phillip was still not there in the bed. This was a very private time, just between the Lord and me.

My vision of the room seemed fuzzy, and I blinked my eyes to clear them. Then, I realized that all the blinking in the world could not clear the room. It was filled with a cloud, and the cloud was not absent from any part of the room. The fact that my body was in a frozen condition was because of the heavy cloud that kept me from moving.

This cloud was the holy presence of the living God. I had asked Him for a visitation, and He had awakened me for that purpose. Years later, I was to learn that what I had seen was the cloud of God's glory.

I lay there and watched the cloud for some indeterminable amount of time. It was everywhere. After a while, I felt something begin to move from the top of my head, and it slowly worked its way all the way through my body. I was so afraid of this physical sensation that I wanted to cry out to Phillip, but I could not. It was only later that I realized that experience was the infilling of the Holy Spirit.

Not knowing at the time what was happening, I did something I will always regret. I asked the Lord to please take it away. I was afraid, I told Him. If He would come back during the day, I would surrender to this experience.

The next thing I knew, it was morning, and everything was back to normal. Some might think this was just a dream, but I know that it was not. I was as conscious then as I am right now. It was perhaps the most real experience I have ever had.

The Return

The next morning, I told Phillip what had happened, and he was dumbfounded. I will let him express his feelings in his own words, but I must say that he made fun of me and did not believe the Lord would come back to me during the day. I was sure He would, and I decided that I would keep all future visitations from my husband, so that he couldn't make fun of me.

That morning, after I saw our two children off to school, I was at the kitchen sink washing dishes. There was a window over the sink, and I was looking out at our backyard. As I completed the task at hand, I was feeling very peaceful and joyous from the night before.

I was a changed person. I felt almost as though I had been born again AGAIN. Words could not describe the feeling. I began to believe that I had actually been filled with the Holy Spirit during the night. If so, the only thing lacking was my prayer language, and I knew it was there for me if I would just yield.

Suddenly, though, I was gripped with fear, because I had the distinct sensation that someone was standing behind me. I remembered that I hadn't locked the kitchen door after the children went out, and I became concerned that someone had slipped into the kitchen. I turned around quickly, expecting to find some intruder there, but there was no one.

I locked the door, caught my breath and went back to my work. But, there it was again. Someone was there. My heart started beating rapidly, and I turned around quickly.

When there was again no one visible behind me in the kitchen, then I remembered the invitation I had issued to the Lord the evening before. He had taken me up on that invitation. I found myself saying, "Yes, Lord, I said I would surrender, and I know why You are here."

I went to my bedroom and got down on my knees. It was different this time. The supernatural experience of the previous evening was not there — only a peace and a knowing that I was already filled. This was the time for me to surrender my tongue to my prayer language and the gift of tongues that comes as a natural outflowing of the infilling of the Holy Spirit. By faith, I simply opened my mouth and began to speak. As the language poured out of my being, I was filled with such joy and peace that I lost all sense of time.

Much later, when I opened my eyes, the presence of the Lord seemed to have dissipated, at least in the way it was before. Now, however, He was within me. The outward presence had left me when our appointed mission was complete. From this day forward, my life would be on a course that I could not control, an adventure of a lifetime.

My experience was a little different from Vivian's:

The Search

After reading those two books, I knew I was on the right track. The difficulty I was still having was believing that so many people were on the wrong track. I had always believed the Bible was true and that miracles were for today, but I had never been in a church that believed and experienced the miracle-working power of God. I felt like Much-Afraid in the Christian classic *Hinds' Feet On High Places* by Hannah Hurnard. She begins: "This is the story of how Much-Afraid escaped from her Fearling relatives and went with the Shepherd to the High Places where 'perfect love casteth out all fear.' Like most of the other families that lived in the Valley of Humiliation, all the Fearlings hated the Chief Shepherd and tried to boycott His servants, and naturally it was a great offense to them that one of their own family should have entered His service. Consequently they did all they could, both by threats and persuasions, to get her out of His employment, and one dreadful day they laid before her the family dictum that she must immediately marry her cousin Craven Fear and settle down respectably among her own people. If she refused to do this of her own free will, they threatened to use force and compel her." [1]

It was clear to me that I had a major decision to make. I could live the rest of my life with the Fearlings, or I could be born again and receive a new set of relatives (allegorically speaking). At this point, I was a successful twenty-seven-year-old CPA with a wife, two children and a dog, but with no real life. I needed to "get a life," as the common expression puts it.

As I began to seek the baptism of the Holy Spirit, I met many people who had received this experience. They seemed to be full of joy and love like no people I had ever met. They were all praying for me, but no one really understood the demonic mental torment, depression, anxiety attacks and borderline insanity that I had experienced for the previous twelve years of my life. I could write a book on this deliverance alone, but that is not the purpose of this particular book.

The Very Public Beginning

One Friday night, after work, a friend of mine and I went to a restaurant to have a cup of coffee. He had been counseling me for several months — without much success. In desperation, I suppose, he asked me, "Phillip, are you sure you are saved? Are you born again?" I had always assumed that I was saved, but one verse of scripture did trouble me:

> *For whoever is ashamed of Me and My words in this adulterous and sinful generation, the Son of Man will also be ashamed of him when He comes in the glory of His Father with the holy angels.*
>
> Mark 8:38

I had never unashamedly confessed Jesus as my Lord. As a matter of fact, I was much more concerned about what people thought about me and about the effects religion might have on my career than I was about my soul. That, however, was about to change.

As my friend continued to talk, I began to listen to the voice of the Holy Spirit, and I couldn't believe what He was telling me to do. It was as though Jesus was standing next to me and smiling as He told me to stand up in the restaurant and confess Him before the people there. Mark 8:38 was burning a hole in my conscience. I knew, even before I stood, that I was about to be changed forever. Right now, as I am writing these words, tears come to my eyes when I remember this wonderful experience with Jesus.

I told my friend that I was ready to receive Jesus.

He said, "Good! Let's go outside and pray."

Then I told him what Jesus told me to do.

He said, "If that's what He says to do, go ahead, Brother!"

So with my three-piece suit and layer upon layer of pride that I was wearing, I stood, trembling on the inside. I raised my voice and hands to get everyone's attention. Then I really began to tremble because all the people in the restaurant, about a hundred of them, none of whom I knew, stopped eating and looked at me in total amazement.

But I couldn't stop now. "I want everyone here to know tonight," I managed, "that I am receiving Jesus Christ as my personal Lord and Savior." Then the Holy Spirit gently spoke to me and told me to fall on my knees and He would give me the words to pray. As I literally fell to my knees, I cried out to God with a loud voice so everyone could hear, "Lord Jesus, please have mercy on my miserable soul. I am a sinner. Please come into my heart and save me."

As I stood to my feet, three or four Christians in the restaurant also stood up and said, "Praise the Lord!" One giant of a man who had been seated across the aisle from us literally picked me up and swung me in a circle. He was exclaiming, "Brother, if you keep that boldness, you will never have any problems from the devil." Those words would prove to be prophetic.

I did not feel bold at all. By now, I was trembling on the outside as well as the inside, and I wondered why I was so afraid when I had just been so bold. But what I was feeling was not fear. It was the power of God, and it was overwhelming.

When I got home that night, Vivian took one look at me and knew that something had happened. My face literally burned for about six months after that, as though I had been sunburned. Every morning, for weeks afterward, I would look in the mirror to see the change in my countenance. I looked much younger and could hardly believe what had happened to me.

The Empowerment

That next morning, I could hear the voice of the Holy Spirit very clearly as He spoke many things to me. The first thing He said to me was, "Why did you wait so long? I have missed fellowshipping with you." He spoke many other personal things to me, but none of the words that He spoke to me were condemning. He never mentioned my sins (which had been legion). He only expressed His love for me. It was as though I was enveloped in a cocoon of love that surrounded me for several feet in every direction. I sensed that the evil spirits (depression, fear and anxiety) that had tormented me for years were still hanging around outside this cocoon, but they could not penetrate it.

That night, as I was visiting with my friend late into the night, he asked me, "What is it that you want?"

I replied that I wanted to receive the baptism of the Holy Spirit.

He said, "Do you believe that you have the faith to receive?"

I said that I did.

He said, "What are you waiting for?"

At this point, I knelt in front of a chair and lifted my hands in the air. Immediately, the Holy Spirit began to descend upon my upper body. My fingers, then my hands, then my arms, and then my face all became numb.

The only way I can describe it is that it was like being shot with warm Novocain.

I began to speak, and my tongue was so thick that I was babbling like a baby. What I was saying was certainly not part of any language, but it felt good, and I was experiencing such a manifest presence of God that I continued on.

Then, in my mind, I asked God to give me a prayer language. At about that same time, the enemy spoke to me and said, "If you don't stop right now, you are going to burst a blood vessel in your neck and die." Indeed, I was praying just that fervently.

But, immediately following the lie of the devil, Jesus spoke to me. He asked, "What happened to you last night?"

In my mind, I replied, "I was born again."

He said, "That's right, and what do you care if you die or not? You will be with Me."

At that instant, a physical gurgling began to erupt in my stomach. I felt it rising, and when it reached my mouth, my tongue literally flipped over, and I heard myself speaking in the most beautiful language I had ever heard.

At the same time, it was as though the top of my head was removed, and my spirit left my body and went into Heaven. This liberty of being out of my body was indescribable. It was a heavenly experience, so only heavenly words could describe it.

I continued speaking in tongues for some time, and I heard the language change at least three times that I could detect. In some strange way, I was a spectator to what was occurring with my body. Slowly, I felt myself descending, even though I did not want to, until the Holy Spirit reached my innermost being and rested there.

After this experience, I thought I could never doubt the power and goodness of God. Years later, however, I found that I had far underestimated the power of the evil one and the power of my flesh. But God even works through our failures.

You Are Either Pregnant or Not

Jesus' conversation with Nicodemus describes how we become pregnant with the Spirit:

> *Jesus answered and said to him, "Truly, truly, I say to you, unless one is born again, he cannot see the kingdom of God."*
> *Nicodemus said to Him, "How can a man be born when he is old? He cannot enter a second time into his mother's womb and be born, can he?"*
> *Jesus answered, "Truly, truly, I say to you, unless one is born of water and the Spirit, he cannot enter into the kingdom of God. That which is born of the flesh is flesh, and that which is born of the Spirit is spirit. Do not marvel that I said to you, 'You must be born again.' The wind blows where it wishes and you hear the sound of it, but do not know where it comes from and where it is going; so is everyone who is born of the Spirit."* John 3:3-8

Nicodemus didn't understand anything about being *Pregnant With Christ*, just as those who have not been born again today do not understand:

*Therefore if any man is in Christ, he is a new crea-
ture; the old things passed away; behold, new things
have come.*   2 Corinthians 5:17

This *"new creature"* is pregnant with the Spirit of
Christ.

Kenneth Hagin explains the new birth as follows:
"Several kinds of deaths are spoken of in the Bible, but
there are three kinds with which we need to familiarize
ourselves: 1. Spiritual Death, 2. Physical Death, 3. Eternal Death, or the second death, which is being cast into
the lake which burneth with fire and brimstone.

"Spiritual Death came to the earth first, then manifested itself in the physical body by destroying it.
Physical Death is but a manifestation of the law which
is at work within, called by Paul *'the law of sin and death'*
(Romans 8:2). When God said to Adam, *'In the day that
thou eatest thereof thou shalt surely die,'* He did not refer to
physical death, but to spiritual death. If man had never
died spiritually, he would not have died physically.
Spiritual death means separation from God. The moment
Adam sinned, he was separated from God, and when
God came in the cool of the day, as was His custom, to
walk and talk with Adam, and called, 'Adam, where art
thou?' Adam said, 'I hid myself.' He was separated from
God.

"Man is now united with the devil. He is an outcast,
an outlaw, driven from the garden with no legal ground
of approach to God. He no longer responds to the call of
God. He responds only to his new nature, or to his new
master. Man is more than a transgressor. He is more than

a lawbreaker and a sinner. Man is spiritually a child of
the devil, and he partakes of his father's nature. This explains why man cannot be saved by conduct. He has to
be born again. If man were not a child of the devil, then
he could just begin to put on the right kind of conduct,
and he'd be all right. But even if he puts on right conduct, he still is a child of the devil and will go to Hell
when he dies — to the lake which burneth with fire and
brimstone, which is the second death. Man cannot stand
in the presence of God as he is — because he has the
nature of his father — the devil. If man is ever saved, he
has to be saved by someone paying the penalty for his
sins, and by someone giving him a new nature." [2]

Of course, Jesus is the one who paid the penalty for
our sins and opened the way for us to receive our new
nature. All we must do is open our hearts by faith and
receive Him as Lord of our lives.

A Woman Knows When She Is Pregnant

A woman knows when she is pregnant. At first, she
just has an inner knowing that something is different.
Her body is changing, and she senses with anticipation
that her whole existence is changing. The world around
her looks different. She feels protective of her condition.
In the same way, when we are *Pregnant With Christ*, we
have a sense of anticipation that something is different.
We see the world through the eyes of Jesus, and it looks
very different.

Can you remember the first day after you were born
again? You woke up to sunlight that was brighter, a sky

that was bluer, and the world had a crisp, clear look and feel to it. Smells were more distinct, and sounds had a new melody all their own. Some of the most ordinary things seemed suddenly extraordinary.

In the same way a pregnant woman feels protective of her body, we who have conceived Christ within us feel very protective that nothing robs us of the joy and thrill of knowing we belong to Him. Such is the first day of pregnancy for a woman, and such is our first day of being *Pregnant With Christ.*

As time goes by, the new mother begins to feel, ever so slightly, a stirring within her womb as the baby moves for the first time. The flutter of that tiny being brings delight, as well as anticipation. It is a promise of things to come. She senses her life will never be the same again.

We Need To Know We Are Pregnant

There is a preparation time. The new mother needs to study and educate herself for the future. If she is wise, she seeks advice from those who have been through this process before, receiving instruction from her elders. She is an eager student.

It would benefit us as believers, who are *Pregnant With Christ,* to seek the same wisdom as the mother-to-be. We have never walked this way before. We need to study the heavenly Father's Instruction Book diligently to educate ourselves for our new role in this birthing process. We cannot continue to walk in old wineskins, because this new wine revelation that God is giving to the Church can only be contained in new wineskins. We must become like Mary, the sister of Martha, who sat at the feet of her Christ to glean from being in His presence. We must listen carefully to the apostles, prophets, pastors, teachers and evangelists the Lord has placed over us, and heed their teaching. In this way, we can prepare for the birthing process.

Our Responsibility

As the birth nears, a woman feels her body becoming heavier. There is a weight upon her that is part of the process. Her movements are more calculated and her preparation more crucial with every waking day. The nights are more uncomfortable as she tries to rest. There is nothing she can do to hide her condition. She feels a heaviness and, at the same time, an excitement that the time is near. She is careful to get the proper amount of rest, to eat the proper foods, to drink the proper drinks, to exercise with discretion, all to protect the precious gift that God has entrusted to her.

In the same way, we have a great responsibility to protect this Christ Child within us through spiritual warfare. Because we are in the ninth month, we are to put on the full armor of God as never before and to stand firm against the schemes of the devil, who would try to kill this Child. We are to stand firm, having our loins girded with truth. We are to put on the breastplate of righteousness, and to have our feet shod with the preparation of the Gospel of peace. We are to take up the shield of faith, that will extinguish the flaming missiles of the evil one that would try to destroy this Child. We are to take the helmet of salvation, and the sword of the Spirit, which is the Word of God, and we are to slay every enemy of this Child. With all prayer and petitions, we are to pray in the Spirit for all of those who are also pregnant with Christ. We will not be ignorant of the schemes of the devil whose only purpose is to destroy this child within us. Instead, we will cast down every evil thought that he places in our minds in opposition to the pure Child within us.

Once, when I was burdened by a number of personal matters and went to the Lord in prayer, He revealed to me that He was trying to get my attention so that He could speak to me about something entirely different than what I wanted to discuss with Him. As I began to pray, I saw Him as the Commander in Chief of His army. He revealed to me how we were hindering this conception process by not looking to Him for our marching orders. He gave commands to His disciples, *"And gathering them together, He commanded them not to leave Jerusalem"* (Acts 1:4). We cannot execute this conception without explicitly following the orders of our Commander in Chief.

The Vision

As I was meditating on this in prayer, I began to see a vision of a multitude of leaders in battle. Only a few had their heads raised looking for their Commander. In each of these whose heads were lifted, there was a stream of light, like a laser, proceeding from Jesus to them. The Lord spoke to me and said that His ministers are hindering His plan by being more concerned about their personal vision and ministry than they are about the overall battle plan of the Commander in Chief. Only a small percentage are truly looking toward their Commander in Chief and have His interests at heart, with no mixture of motives or selfish ambition.

As the vision continued, more and more of the multitude of warriors began to look upward. As they did, more streams of light came downward, until there was finally only one brilliant light. At this point, I realized the warriors had come into unity, the same unity for which Jesus had prayed:

> *And the glory which Thou hast given Me I have given to them; that they may be one, just as We are one.*   John 17:22

It suddenly occurred to me how simple this unity really is. As we each lift our heads to look upon Him and His grace, glory and love, we become partakers of this glory and automatically become one in Him. The beginning of this process started at conception.

The Process

A.W. Tozer gave an appropriate analogy to this vision in his writings fifty years ago: "Someone may fear that we are magnifying private religion out of all proportion, that the 'us' of the New Testament is being displaced by a selfish 'I.' Has it ever occurred to you that one hundred pianos all tuned to the same fork are

automatically tuned to each other? They are of one ac-
cord by being tuned, not to each other, but to another
standard to which one must individually bow. So one
hundred worshipers meeting together, each one looking away to Christ, are in heart nearer to each other than
they could possibly be were they to become 'unity' conscious and turn their eyes away from God to strive for
closer fellowship." [3]

The Vision Continued

As I continued to seek the Lord in prayer, He showed
me the weapons of warfare His warriors were wearing.
As the warriors lifted their heads toward His glory, the
brilliant colors of the weapons glittered in the light. His
glory reflected off these weapons, and no demon or
fleshly thought could come near them.

Then I saw others who had on the full armor, but their
heads were not lifted upward. All of their weapons were
a dull gray and were of no use to them. I asked the Lord
what this meant, and He said that they had taken up
their weapons (at one point in time) with their eyes on
Him, but they had later taken their eyes off Him. It occurred to me why many Christians and even entire
denominations have knowledge but are totally defeated
in warfare. For instance, many read the Word of God
but have no illumination or revelation of what it is truly
saying.

Only the Commander-in-Chief can open our hearts to
understand His Word. Many understand mentally the
helmet of salvation, but they have no heart knowledge.

They even bring others into their mental knowledge of salvation, but still they are never born again of God's Spirit. Many believe they have girded their loins with truth, and yet their truth is a combination of truths, legalism, cultural Christianity and a self-fulfillment Gospel that has nothing in common with the truth of God's Word. Many even pray, but they pray with wrong motives, in unbelief and with meaningless repetition, which is profitable to no one.

All of these had on the dull gray armor of warfare that was in no way profitable to the conception process and even hindered it, because their eyes were not on their Commander in Chief. These backslidden Christians are not looking expectantly for their Commander in Chief, and they will be left behind as He descends with a shout to receive His pregnant ones.

1. *Hinds' Feet on High Places,* Hannah Hurnard, Living Books, Tyndale House Publishers, Wheaton, IL, 1977, Chapter 1, pp. 17, 19.
2. *The New Birth*, Kenneth F. Hagin, Rhema Bible Church, 1975, Kenneth Hagin Ministries, Inc., Tulsa, OK, pp. 10,11.
3. *The Pursuit of God*, A.W. Tozer, Christian Publications, Camp Hill, PA, 1982, 1993, p. 87.

Chapter 3

The Abortionist

*For this reason, rejoice, O heavens and you who
dwell in them. Woe to the earth and the sea, because the devil has come down to you, having great
wrath, knowing that he has only a short time.*
                                    Revelation 12:12

The intensity of the battle to kill the child within you
will be greater now than at any other time in history.
Satan knows that we are pregnant with Christ, and he
will use all of his power in trying to kill this Child within
us. Jesus said, *"The thief comes only to steal, and kill, and
destroy"* (John 10:10).

Rick Joyner received a vision from the Lord which
he recorded in his book *The Final Quest*: "The demonic
army was so large that it stretched as far as I could see.
It was separated into divisions, with each carrying a
different banner. The foremost divisions marched
under the banners of Pride, Self-righteousness, Respectability, Selfish Ambition, Unrighteous Judgment and
Jealousy. There were many more of these evil divisions
beyond my scope of vision, but those in the vanguard
of this terrible horde from Hell seemed to be the most

powerful. The leader of this army was the Accuser of the Brethren himself.

"The weapons carried by this horde were also named. The swords were named Intimidation; the spears were named Treachery; and the arrows were named Accusation, Gossip, Slander and Faultfinding. Scouts and smaller companies of demons with such names as Rejection, Bitterness, Impatience, Unforgiveness and Lust were sent in advance of this army to prepare for the main attack." [1]

Satan's primary strategy in destroying this Child will be the one we have already seen recorded throughout the Bible. His plan has always been to destroy the seed of God at or near birth. Once, he even conceived the bizarre plan of totally polluting the human race:

> *Now it came about, when men began to multiply on the face of the land, and daughters were born to them, that the sons of God saw that the daughters of men were beautiful; and they took wives for themselves, whomever they chose.*
>
> *Then the LORD said, "My spirit shall not strive with man forever, because he also is flesh; nevertheless his days shall be one hundred and twenty years."*
>
> *The Nephilim were on the earth in those days, and also afterward, when the sons of God came in to the daughters of men, and they bore children to them. Those were the mighty men who were of old, men of renown.*
>
> *Then the LORD saw that the wickedness of man was great on the earth, and that every intent of the thoughts of his heart was only evil continually. And*

the LORD was sorry that He had made man on the
earth, and He was grieved in His heart.
But Noah found favor in the eyes of the LORD.

Genesis 6:1-6 and 8

Dr. David Yonggi Cho states in his book *Prayer That Brings Revival:* "Satan's trick was to pollute the human race so that the seed of woman (Jesus Christ) could not be pure. Therefore, He could not bring destruction to his [Satan's] kingdom. Yet, God had one man who had not been polluted. One family found favor in the sight of God. So Noah was the means by which the human race was saved from total and complete destruction.

"Satan continued his opposition by trying to destroy Israel. Then, he tried to destroy the Christ Child. Finally, he hung the Son of God on the cross. Yet, the cross was not the end – through the death of our precious Lord on the cross, Satan was defeated by Jesus Christ. Because of the death and the resurrection of Jesus Christ, we also have been given authority over Satan and his works. Therefore, we are more than conquerors through Him who loved us." [2]

The History of the Enemy's Battle Plan

Satan was present when God called Abraham and promised to bless him and all the families of the earth through him. The enemy overheard those covenant words. He also heard these covenant words:

On that day the LORD made a covenant with Abraham, saying, "To your descendants I have

*given this land, from the river of Egypt as far as the
great river, the river Euphrates."*   Genesis 15:18

Satan knew that if he could prevent Abraham from
having a child, he could thwart the plan of God to bless
His chosen people. We know this plan failed:

*In order that in Christ Jesus the blessing of Abra-
ham might come to the Gentiles, so that we might
receive the promise of the Spirit through faith.*
*Now the promises were spoken to Abraham and to
his seed. He does not say, "And to seeds," as refer-
ring to many, but rather to one, "And to your seed,"
that is, Christ.*   Galatians 3:14 and 16

The seed of Abraham was Christ, and we are now
pregnant with this same seed, and the Child is about to
be delivered once and for all.

Satan probably thought that he succeeded when Abraham had Ishmael by Sarah's maid Hagar, but God had
other plans. Supernaturally, Sarah became pregnant with
Isaac, the child of promise. This seed that was born in faith
prospered, and we now have the promise of Galatians 4:28,
"And you brethren, like Isaac, are children of promise."

Satan does not change his strategy. He is very persis-
tent. This is one of his greatest weapons. Therefore, we
need perseverance and patience to combat him. After
he had tried to prevent Abraham and Sarah from having a child, he did the exact same thing to Isaac and
Rebekah. She, too, was barren, but again God intervened.

And Isaac prayed to the LORD on behalf of his wife,
because she was barren; and the LORD answered him
and Rebekah his wife conceived.   Genesis 25:21

Rebekah had twins. The firstborn, Esau, was a type of
the flesh, and the second, Jacob, was a type of the Spirit
or promise. I'm sure Satan was now hoping that the
blessing would pass to Esau as he had hoped it would
pass to Ishmael, but the sovereignty and providence of
God always brings about His preordained plan.

When that didn't work, Satan tried to prevent Jacob
and Rachel from having a child. Rachel, too, was barren, but she prayed to the Lord, and God answered her:

Then God remembered Rachel, and God gave heed
to her and opened her womb.   Genesis 30:22

The seed of God's promise continued until the time
of Moses, when Satan again raised his ugly head, much
more viciously. He did not know which Israelite would
deliver the children of Israel, so he tried to kill all the
male children through Pharaoh. Pharaoh's vicious plan
is recorded in the book of Exodus:

Then Pharaoh commanded all his people, saying,
"Every son who is born you are to cast into the
Nile, and every daughter you are to keep alive."
Now a man from the house of Levi went and mar-
ried a daughter of Levi. And the woman conceived
and bore a son; and when she saw that he was beau-
tiful, she hid him for three months. But when she

could hide him no longer, she got him a wicker bas-
ket and covered it over with tar and pitch. Then
she put the child into it, and set it among the reeds
by the bank of the Nile. Exodus 1:22-2:3

Since God's chosen deliverer, Moses, escaped Satan's
death plan, I'm sure Satan thought he would fill Moses
with the ways of the world in Egypt, so that he would
have no concern for God or His people. Of course we
know the rest of the story. Satan's plan did not work
with Moses, and his plan will not work against those
believers currently *Pregnant With Christ!*

By faith Moses, when he had grown up, refused to
be called the son of Pharaoh's daughter; choosing
rather to endure ill-treatment with the people of
God, than to enjoy the passing pleasures of sin; con-
sidering the reproach of Christ greater riches than
the treasures of Egypt; for he was looking to the
reward. By faith he left Egypt, not fearing the wrath
of the king; for he endured, as seeing Him who is
unseen. Hebrews 11:24-27

Following his same strategy, Satan tried to prevent
Samson from being born:

And there was a certain man of Zorah, of the fam-
ily of the Danites, whose name was Manoah; and
his wife was barren and had borne no children. Then
the angel of the LORD appeared to the woman, and

said to her, "Behold now, you are barren and have
borne no children, but you shall conceive and give
birth to a son.   Judges 13:2-3

We are all familiar with the miracles that Samson performed, in defeating the Philistines with supernatural
strength. He did so against Satan's wishes.

I'm sure Satan did not want to see the birth of Samuel, but God had other plans:

And Hannah rose after eating and drinking in
Shiloh. Now Eli the priest was sitting on the seat
by the doorpost of the temple of the LORD. And she,
greatly distressed, prayed to the LORD and wept bit-
terly. And she made a vow and said, "O LORD of
hosts, if Thou wilt indeed look on the affliction of
Thy maidservant and remember me, and not forget
Thy maidservant, but wilt give Thy maidservant a
son, then I will give him to the LORD all the days of
his life, and a razor shall never come on his head."
                                                   1 Samuel 1:9-11

Samuel was born and became a great prophet of the
Lord, again destroying Satan's plan.

Satan's plan was not working, but he didn't give up.
He certainly did not want John the Baptist, the great
prophet and preacher of repentance, who would usher
in the coming of the Lord, to be born. For this reason,
Zacharias and Elizabeth also had difficulty conceiving a
child:

> *And they had no child, because Elizabeth was bar-*
> *ren, and they were both advanced in years.*
>
> Luke 1:7

Zacharias was in the temple one day performing his service to the Lord when an angel appeared to him and said, *"Do not be afraid, Zacharias, for your petition has been heard, and your wife Elizabeth will bear you a son, and you will give him the name John"* (Luke 1:13). Zacharias argued with the angel (this is not a good idea):

> *And Zacharias said to the angel, "How shall I know*
> *this for certain? For I am an old man, and my wife*
> *is advanced in years."*
> *And the angel answered and said to him, "I am*
> *Gabriel, who stands in the presence of God; and I*
> *have been sent to speak to you, and to bring you*
> *this good news. And behold, you shall be silent and*
> *unable to speak until the day when these things take*
> *place, because you did not believe my words, which*
> *shall be fulfilled in their proper time."*
>
> Luke 1:18-20

Zacharias and Elizabeth remind us of Abraham and Sarah, and God also moved upon them supernaturally to fulfill His purposes.

So now we have come to the fullness of time, and the Son of God is born through a virgin. Satan couldn't stop the birth, so he tried to kill the Child in infancy, the same way he tried to kill Moses. God protected the Child from Herod by speaking to the wise men:

> *And having been warned by God in a dream not to*
> *return to Herod, they departed for their own coun-*
> *try by another way.*   Matthew 2:12

He also spoke to Joseph to protect the Child:

> *Now when they had departed, behold, an angel of*
> *the Lord appeared to Joseph in a dream, saying,*
> *"Arise and take the Child and His mother, and flee*
> *to Egypt, and remain there until I tell you; for Herod*
> *is going to search for the Child to destroy him."*
>   Matthew 2:13

In an attempt to kill the great deliverer, Moses, Satan
entered into Pharaoh, and he had all the male children
of his day killed. Now Satan entered into Herod, and he
also killed all the male children. This was an attempt to
kill the One who will ultimately destroy him:

> *Then when Herod saw that he had been tricked by*
> *the magi, he became very enraged, and sent and*
> *slew all the male children who were in Bethlehem*
> *and in all its environs, from two years old and un-*
> *der, according to the time which he had ascertained*
> *from the magi.*   Matthew 2:16

We also see Satan warring with this Child propheti-
cally and with His mother:

> *And a great sign appeared in heaven: a woman*
> *clothed with the sun, and the moon under her feet,*

*and on her head a crown of twelve stars; and she
was with child; and she cried out, BEING IN
LABOR AND IN PAIN TO GIVE BIRTH. And
another sign appeared in heaven: and behold, a great
red dragon having seven heads and ten horns, and
on his heads were seven diadems. And his tail swept
away a third of the stars of heaven, and threw them
to the earth. And the dragon stood before the woman
who was about to give birth, SO THAT WHEN
SHE GAVE BIRTH HE MIGHT DEVOUR HER
CHILD. And she gave birth to a son, a male child,
who is to rule all the nations with a rod of iron;
and her child was caught up to God and to His
throne.* Revelation 12:1-5

Satan's Current Battle Plan

Twice, then, Satan has killed many thousands of innocent children, trying to prevent God's plan from being
consummated. Both times these evil plans centered
around destroying a child at birth or shortly thereafter.
Now, in his third and final attempt, Satan is trying,
through abortion, to prevent the birthing process of the
sons of God and the second coming of the Lord Jesus
Christ.

If Satan was evil in the destruction of the children in
Moses' and in Jesus' day, how much more vicious will
he be in this day and hour, knowing that he is about to
be cast into the lake of fire? Satan knows that God is
restoring all things to His Church and that the book of
Acts is only a shadow of what is to come when the full

functionality of the fivefold ministry gifts is restored to the Church. Satan, therefore, has been successful in destroying many potential apostles and prophets, evangelists, pastors and teachers through the evils of abortion. He also has destroyed many through the evil flood of drug addiction throughout the world today. This is his last chance.

Instead of doing spiritual warfare with principalities and powers and defeating them with the mighty weapons God has given us, we have often attempted to fight the enemy by fleshly means, and we have failed. This last-day Church will learn to do spiritual warfare as directed by the Great Warrior Himself.

I could not agree more with the spirit of the revelation which Rick Joyner received, as recorded in his book *Overcoming the Accuser*. He said: "In 1989, I had an experience in which I was caught up into the presence of the Lord, and in this experience I was a witness to the anger of the Lord over abortion. To my surprise, His anger was directed at the Church and not the heathen. He declared that if the Church had not aborted the spiritual seeds that He had planted in her, for missions, outreaches, and even the simple witness to our neighbors, then the heathen would not be living in such darkness and would not be aborting the natural seed. He said that the Church was aborting the spiritual seed for all the same reasons that the heathen were aborting their unborn — because of our selfishness, because these (children) would be expensive and we did not think we could afford them, because we did not want to give them our time. He affirmed that judgment would come upon our country because of the evil of abortion, but that He was going to start with His own household first!" [3]

Many of you who are reading this can think back on your life and remember many times when Satan has tried to kill you. This was because he knew you would have a part in ushering in the second coming of Christ. He knew that you would have the great honor and privilege of being *Pregnant With Christ* in the ninth month. My own mother had five miscarriages before I was born, and she was late in years by the time she gave birth to me. I was the only child. Satan tried to kill me at birth, and he has tried to kill me many times since then, even as he has tried to kill many of you. You must realize your calling for this hour and know that Satan will try to kill the Christ in you, for he is an abortionist.

Jesus tells us clearly some of the things that will occur before our pregnancy comes to full term. For instance, Matthew 24:19 says, *"But woe to those who are with child and to those who nurse babes in those days!"* Since we are *Pregnant With Christ* and in the ninth month, the opposition against us from the abortionist will be greater than for any previous generation of Christians. Satan's primary weapon will be the attempt to destroy the love in God's people. Jesus said in Matthew 24:12-13, *"And because lawlessness is increased, most people's love will grow cold. But the one who endures to the end, he shall be saved."* In other words, the one who does not allow the enemy to abort this Christ Child will be saved.

One of the main weapons to counteract this attack of lawlessness against the Church is the absolute unequivocal revelation of the goodness of God, and in the same proportion, the evil of the abortionist.

Another great weapon that Satan has been successful in using against God's people is bringing havoc, disease, distress, fear, etc., upon the people of God and then convincing them these things came from God. Because of the great distress that Satan will attempt to bring upon all expectant believers, we must be absolutely assured of the goodness of God in the days ahead. As one songwriter has well penned, "God is good, all the time, and all the time, God is good."

The great dichotomy of this final age is that not only are we *Pregnant With Christ*, but that Satan is giving birth to his child at the same time. This is the reason for the cataclysmic warfare that has already begun. Evil is becoming more wicked, and good is becoming more pure.

The irony is that the very evil the abortionist is attempting to bring about will return to him in exactly the same measure and proportion he intended to bring upon God's children. Remember that Satan was not able to destroy the infant Moses because of the protection of God. The vessel Satan attempted to use in his murderous plan was Pharaoh. In the end, all of the firstborn children of Egypt were destroyed, including Pharaoh's. The evil Satan intended on the elect of God was, in fact, delivered upon the enemies of God.

We see this theme occurring again and again in the Bible. Another case was with Haman and Mordecai. It was Haman, not Mordecai, who hung from the gallows, after his plot to hang Mordecai had backfired.

Satan's offspring will be destroyed and will receive the same punishment he receives. The offspring of which I speak is the Antichrist.

And then that lawless one will be revealed whom
the Lord will slay with the breath of His mouth and
bring to an end by the appearance of His coming.
2 Thessalonians 2:8

And the beast was seized, and with him the false
prophet who performed the signs in his presence,
by which he deceived those who had received the
mark of the beast and those who worshiped his im-
age; these two were thrown alive into the lake of
fire which burns with brimstone.
Revelation 19:20

And, of course, the abortionist himself will suffer the
same fate:

And the devil who deceived them was thrown into
the lake of fire and brimstone, where the beast and
the false prophet are also; and they will be tormented
day and night forever and ever.
Revelation 20:10

What a day of rejoicing that will be for the pregnant
ones!

Some time ago, I was to preach in Pensacola, Florida,
in a church that has been experiencing revival, and I was
very excited to have the opportunity to minister in that
revival atmosphere. God did many wonderful things in
His people while I was there, but not before there was a
battle. At 5:00 o'clock of the morning we were to leave
Atlanta for Pensacola, I received a call from our daugh-

ter Jenny (who is also in the ministry in Greensboro, North Carolina). Suffering from severe headaches, she was on her way to the emergency room of a local hospital. I immediately began to pray in the Spirit for her.

Jenny called back about six to say that the attending physician thought she might have meningitis. He wanted to do a spinal tap. Knowing the severity of the diagnosis and the risk involved in doing the procedure, I told Jenny to wait until I had prayed further.

Almost immediately, I knew this was a direct attack from the abortionist and that I had power over him through Jesus. As I continued to pray in the Spirit, the Holy Spirit spoke to me that the diagnosis was incorrect.

When Jenny called back, I told her not to have the spinal tap and to go home. She called back about an hour later, after she had spoken to her personal physician, and it turned out that she had some type of unusual virus. She was fine within twenty-four hours.

We will need all the gifts of the Holy Spirit to combat the abortionist in the ninth month of this pregnancy. In this case, I was blessed to receive a word of knowledge when Jenny's life was on the line. We departed for Pensacola on schedule, and had victorious services. It had not come without a battle with the abortionist.

Endnotes

1. *The Final Quest*, Rick Joyner, Whitaker House, New Kensington, PA, 1996, p. 16.
2. *Prayer That Brings Revival*, Dr. David Yonggi Cho, Creation House, Lake Mary, FL., 1998, Chapter 1, p. 17.
3. *Overcoming the Accuser*, Rick Joyner, Morningstar Publications, Charlotte, NC, 1996, p. 50.

Chapter 4

The Revealing

For the anxious longing of the creation waits eagerly for THE REVEALING of the sons of God.

Romans 8:19

Not long after natural conception occurs, the anatomy of a woman begins to change. It happens slowly at first, but then the pace picks up about the sixth month. Even if, for some reason, the mother desires to keep her condition secret, soon everyone recognizes that she is indeed pregnant. Later, when a woman is in her ninth month of pregnancy, it is extremely difficult for her to hide that fact. As much as she may try to conceal her condition, it is nearly impossible.

As Christians, we may try not to look funny to the world, but in the days ahead we will look funny, whether we like it or not. Backslidden and carnal Christians will malign us because of our radical condition, which can no longer be hidden. Before this baby is birthed, the world will recognize the sons of God.

Paul wrote to the Corinthian believers:

*So that you are not lacking in any gift, awaiting
eagerly the revelation of our Lord Jesus Christ.*
                                            1 Corinthians 1:7

He is in us, and this fact will be revealed clearly to us
and also to the world around us. Before Jesus comes to
take His Bride, the world will know who we are. We are
all familiar with a deceived subculture in our midst that
has "come out of the closet" in recent years. It is time for
the true sons of God to do the same, so that we can be
recognized by everyone.

I can remember Vivian being pregnant. She was always petite, and when she was expecting, she was a little
self-conscious about her size. Personally, I wasn't looking at her size; I was looking at the glow on her
countenance. I was well aware of the price she was paying and would pay for carrying our child, just as God is
very much aware of the price we are paying in this ninth
month of our pregnancy by the Holy Spirit. We may look
funny to the world, but we will be precious to the Husband, and the Husband is Christ.

The book of Acts is only a shadow of what is to come.
The latter rain will be far greater than the former. Again,
Paul wrote:

*When Christ, who is our life, is revealed, then you
also will be revealed with Him in glory.*
                                            Colossians 3:4

As more and more of Christ is revealed in and through
us, more and more of His glory will be manifested in

His sons and daughters. From the time God first poured out His Spirit on the Day of Pentecost, the world began to recognize something different about His sons. Later, however, especially during the Dark Ages, it became nearly impossible to distinguish between the sons of God and the sons of the evil one.

America's Condition Will Be Revealed

Today, here in our nation, it is sometimes very difficult to recognize the true sons of God. The Church in America is so cultural that we have deceived ourselves into believing that the structure we have on the corner of Main and Broad Streets, with the pastor's name and time of services displayed prominently on a directory on the front lawn, is actually "the Church." Even a cursory reading of the New Testament quickly reveals that this is not true. It is time for God's apostles and prophets to raise their voices and expose this great hypocrisy.

Way back in 1925, Frank Bartleman addressed this same issue: "The world is the field; the true Church is the treasure — like a kernel in a shell, but the great nominal Church, the ecclesiastical in each generation, is also like a field in which the true mystical Church — the living Church — like a treasure, is hidden. Instead of delight in the pure Word, prayer and worship, a love for souls and zeal for good works, there come entertainment, programs, musicals, sensationalism and oratory. These things have no place in essential, true Christianity, but are professionalism — flesh! Most meetings can only be kept alive now by continuous entertainment, professional evangelism and a strong social spirit." [1]

The backslidden cultural church in America, which is really not "the Church" at all, will persecute the true Church as the true sons of God are revealed and begin to worship together. Some of the members of backslidden churches, which have been held in bondage to man and to a social gospel, will begin to see the freedom, joy, power and love these new radical Christians are experiencing, and they will leave the bondage of tradition and religion to experience the freedom of the Spirit of God. This will cause an uproar because they will take their pocketbooks with them. This will be very similar to what happened in the first-century Church:

> *For a certain man named Demetrius, a silversmith, who made silver shrines of Artemis, was bringing no little business to the craftsmen; these he gathered together with the workmen of similar trades, and said, "Men, you know that our prosperity depends upon this business. And you see and hear that not only in Ephesus, but in almost all of Asia, this Paul has persuaded and turned away a considerable number of people, saying that gods made with hands are no gods at all. And not only is there danger that this trade of ours fall into disrepute, but also that the temple of the great goddess Artemis be regarded as worthless and that she whom all of Asia and the world worship should even be dethroned from her magnificence."* Acts 19:24-27

God's Shepherd's Will Also Be Revealed

In the same way the unregenerate and backslidden preachers of our day will cry out. Their message will be, "Men, you know that our prosperity depends upon this business." They will also say, "This trade of ours may fall into disrepute." God is about to uncover the greed and hypocrisy of these false preachers, but they will only cry out because they have lost their trade and the money they have extorted from the innocent. Jesus warned us of these false shepherds who know nothing of true worship and prayer:

> *And He began to teach and say to them, "Is it not written, "My house shall be called a house of prayer for all the nations'? But you have made it a robbers' den."*   Mark 11:17

We are about to see things greater than those recorded in the book of Acts, as the world and the church begin to recognize the true sons of God. Let us review a few of the things that happened then, so that we might prepare ourselves in faith for what God is about to do through us. Notice the radical, supernatural element present in all these events:

In Acts 2, Peter, drunk in the Holy Spirit, stood and declared with great boldness the Gospel of Jesus Christ, and three thousand people were saved. Less than two months prior to this, Peter had tried to kill a man, and he had also denied Christ. When he swung at Malchus, he meant to split his head open. Fortunately, he missed and only cut off his ear. Jesus, of course, healed the ear.

In Acts 3, Peter commanded a man who had been lame from his mother's womb to walk. The man stood upright and began *"walking and leaping and praising God."*

In Acts 4, the disciples prayed, and the place where they had gathered was shaken by the power of God.

In Acts 5, Peter confronted Ananias and Sapphira about lying to the Holy Spirit. They both immediately fell down dead. In that same chapter, one of the most remarkable things recorded in the Bible happened. The sick were carried out in the street so that Peter's shadow might fall on them and heal them. Later, the apostles were thrown into jail, but an angel of the Lord came to them in the night, opened the gates of the prison and set them free.

In Acts 7, as Stephen was being stoned, he saw the heavens opened, the glory of God, and Jesus standing at His right hand.

In Acts 8, Philip was translated by the Holy Spirit from Gaza to Azotus, a distance of about twenty miles. This gives the famous phrase from Star Trek, "Beam me up, Scottie," new meaning.

In Acts 9, a bright light from Heaven knocked Saul to the ground and temporarily blinded him while Jesus spoke to him.

In Acts 10, an angel spoke to Cornelius and told him to send men to Joppa to bring Peter to his house. There, Peter received the vision from the Lord, letting him know that the Gospel was for Gentiles as well as Jews.

In Acts 12, Peter was imprisoned, but as the church prayed, an angel released him from the jail.

In Acts 13, Elymas the magician was opposing the Gospel, and the apostle Paul told him that he would become blind. Immediately, he could not see.

In Acts 14, as Paul was preaching, he perceived that a man who had been lame from his mother's womb had faith to be healed. He told the man to stand up, and immediately the lame man began to walk.

In Acts 16, after being beaten and thrown into jail, Paul and Silas were praying and singing hymns around midnight, when God caused an earthquake to come so that the prison doors were opened, and the chains of everyone in the prison were unfastened.

In Acts 19, handkerchiefs or aprons were carried from the body of Paul to the sick, and diseases left them and evil spirits went out of them.

This is only a small sampling of the things that occurred in the book of Acts (not to mention the many miracles that were never recorded). All of this was "the former rain," and we are about to see greater miracles than these, as Jesus begins to reveal the sons of God to the world.

Throughout the history of God's covenant people in both the Old and New Testaments, the Lord has chosen to appear to select individuals or groups of individuals. For example, Mary Magdalene, although she had been such a sinner, was the first person to see the Lord after His resurrection. I believe that He will begin to appear with increasing frequency to many of those whose hearts are directed toward Him, until He finally appears to all with a shout and the voice of the archangel and the trumpet of God.

Many apostles, prophets and otherwise pregnant saints are already beginning to experience visions, dreams and angelic visitations in increasing numbers. God has a time for everything. He is a God of order. Jesus said:

> *Therefore all the generations from Abraham to David are fourteen generations; and from David to the deportation to Babylon fourteen generations; and from the deportation to Babylon to the time of Christ fourteen generations.*   Matthew 1:17

God orders the times today in the same way He established the various Jewish feasts to be observed on a particular day in a set month. These feasts were given to the Church to teach us of God's redemptive plan in Christ.

Even as these feasts are celebrated by God's covenant people at times which He Himself has set, they are being fulfilled in the Messiah.

The Bible is full of types and shadows that reveal to God's saints His overall plan. Throughout the Bible, we read that He is the God of Abraham, Isaac and Jacob. I see Abraham as a shadow of the Pentecostal Movement, Isaac as a shadow of the Charismatic Movement, Jacob as a shadow of the Renewal Movement, and the twelve patriarchs as a shadow of the coming Saints Movement. This is my own personal feeling, so please grant me some liberty in what I am about to say. I do not claim that it is necessarily a revelation from the Holy Spirit. As you read it, however, I believe that you, too, will see some similarities.

Abraham (The Pentecostal Movement)

First, let us look at Abraham and compare him to the modern-day Pentecostal Movement which began at the turn of the century. This movement was fathered by Charles Parham and William Seymour.

Abraham was, first of all, the father of our faith. He had no example to follow. The Bible says that he had to go out on a journey, not knowing exactly where he was going. Abraham also was called upon to offer up his only son as a sacrifice to God. In this way, he was severely tested, because he was to be an example to us all.

In the same way, Charles Parham and William Seymour had no example to follow in their movement except the book of Acts, and that example was nearly two thousand years old. These two men were also severely tested in their faith. For the most part, the church world did not receive them because others could not understand their walk of faith that produced supernatural signs that had not occurred in such a magnitude in nearly two thousand years. Because of this, those "founding fathers" paid a price that is difficult for us to identify with. Many of those early Pentecostal believers lost their jobs and could not find work simply because they were Pentecostal.

God had said to Abram:

> "No longer shall your name be called Abram, but your name shall be called Abraham; for I will make you the father of a multitude of nations, and I will

make you exceedingly fruitful, and I will make na-
tions of you, and kings shall come forth from you."
                                        Genesis 17:5-6

In the same way, a kingdom of priests has come from
those early Pentecostals who paid the price in prayer,
persecution and persistence so that we might experience
the blessing of Pentecost today. The largest churches now
in existence in the world have arisen within the Pentecostal, Charismatic and Renewal Movements.

The Lord appeared to Abraham on many occasions.
He appeared to him as Melchizedek the priest. He appeared to him at the oaks of Mamre in the heat of the
day. He appeared to him as "the Angel of the Lord." He
appeared to him as the ram caught in the thicket. He
appeared to him as God Almighty.

The Lord also appeared to Frank Bartleman and Edward Boehmer on July 3, 1905. Rick Joyner recorded the
event: "On July 3, Bartleman and Boehmer were in a hall
in Pasadena praying when the burden became almost
unbearable for them, and they cried out like women giving birth. When the burden finally lifted, they just sat
for a while, enjoying the calm that enveloped them. Suddenly the Lord Jesus revealed Himself, standing between
them. They did not dare to move. Love swept over them,
and they felt as if a burning fire went through them. As
Bartleman later wrote:

" 'My whole being seemed to flow down before Him,
like wax before the fire. I lost all consciousness of time
or space, being conscious only of His wonderful presence. I worshipped at His feet. It seemed a veritable

Mount of Transfiguration. I was lost in the pure spirit. The Lord had said nothing to us, but only overwhelmed our spirits by His presence. He had come to strengthen and assure us for His service. We knew now we were workers with Him, fellowshippers of His sufferings in the ministry of "soul travail." Real soul travail is just as definite in the Spirit as natural human birth pains. The simile is almost perfect in its sameness. No soul is ever born without this. All true revivals of salvation come this way.' " [2]

Abraham was a great intercessor, and in Genesis we find him interceding for Sodom and Gomorrah (see Genesis 18). He began by asking God not to destroy the city if there were fifty righteous found there. When God agreed, Abraham then changed his plea to then forty, then thirty, then twenty. Finally, the conversation became even more intense:

> *Then he [Abraham] said, "Oh may the Lord not be*
> *angry, and I shall speak only this once; suppose ten*
> *are found there?"*
> *And He said, I will not destroy it on account of the*
> *ten."*   Genesis 18:32

We know, of course, that not even ten righteous people were found in those cities, and God destroyed them.

The early Pentecostals were known for their intercessory prayer meetings. Sometimes they prayed all night for souls to be saved and for an outpouring of God's Spirit. They have left us a great legacy.

Isaac (The Charismatic Movement)

Abraham was already a hundred years old when his son Isaac was born. In the same way, the Pentecostal Movement was old already when the Charismatic Movement was birthed in the late sixties and early seventies. Unlike Abraham, Isaac had an example.

We know that Isaac was the child of promise, and he received all that Abraham had. *"Now Abraham gave all that he had to Isaac"* (Genesis 25:5). Because of that, I suppose we could say that Isaac was somewhat spoiled compared to Abraham. Those of us who were swept into the Kingdom through the outpouring of the Holy Spirit in what is now called the Charismatic Movement cannot identify with the pain and sacrifice the early Pentecostals went through. In some arenas, it became almost fashionable to speak in tongues. Yes, we received persecution, but not to the degree of our fathers in the faith.

We were, like Isaac, children of promise, and the gifts we received were the gifts of the Holy Spirit that were restored to the Church. In some cases, we acted like spoiled children too. We sometimes misused and even abused the gifts God gave us, and this caused confusion in the Church. It was not that the gifts were not authentic; it was that our flesh was very real. In the end, God began to remove His blessing from those who were no longer praying, fasting and living a holy life and who no longer cared for the lost, but only cared about reaching another spiritual "high." Yet, we have much to be thankful for. It was a wonderful time.

Jacob (The Renewal Movement)

Just when it appeared that the Holy Spirit revival was dead, God opened the womb, as He had with Rebekah when Jacob was born, and sent us another move of His Spirit.

God met Jacob at Bethel (which literally means "The House of God"), and later Jacob returned to Bethel. There, he wrestled with God and prevailed. He dreamed and saw the angels of God ascending and descending on a ladder to Heaven.

Jacob then suffered many trials at the hands of his father-in-law Laban, and he had problems with his children. In the end, he saw God face-to-face.

The Renewal Movement, which the Church is now experiencing, was birthed in a period of great struggle, even as Jacob wrestled with God. Many Charismatics and Pentecostals had become disillusioned with their movements, and, in some instances, had returned to a more formal model of worship with little or no genuine revival. Others simply backslid and returned to sin. Many turned to a sophisticated professionalism, often using carnal principles of church growth and leadership, principles that were no different from those used by many corporate executives.

Frank Bartleman aptly described a similar carnality found at the turn of the century when the great Pentecostal Revival was beginning. He quoted another writer: "The moment we covet a large following and rejoice in the crowd that is attracted by our presentation of what we consider truth, and have not a greater desire to see the natures of individuals changed according to the divine plan, we start to travel the same road of apostasy." [3]

Many of those who had tasted the Pentecostal/Charismatic experience went back to "traditional" churches, thus exchanging a life and liberty in the Spirit for respectability and consistency. They seemed to be totally unaware of Satan's plan to rob them of their first love and the power that accompanies that love. They were again impressed with eloquent sermonettes, forgetting that the Kingdom of God is not manifested in words, but in power. They substituted programs and methodology for their personal relationship with the Holy Spirit. Such substitutes are about to be burned up by the purifying fire of the Holy Spirit.

Some Pentecostal/Charismatic believers, of course, remained faithful and continued their walk with the Lord. Overall, the Charismatic/Pentecostal Church in America desperately needed a fresh touch of God. We needed to come back to Bethel.

God is ever growing the Child within us, so when we came back to Bethel, we did not return to the Pentecostal or Charismatic Movement per se. What He now gave us went much further.

Jacob had a revelation of Jesus Christ that Isaac had not received. He saw God face-to-face at Peniel. He also saw Jesus in the ladder dream. Jesus was the ladder, with the angels of God ascending and descending upon Him. In the same way, God is pouring fresh revelation upon His Church through the Renewal Movement.

This simple revelation of who we are in Christ can be a catalyst that will cause us to walk as sons of God, so the world will recognize us. But this revelation, like all true revelation, causes us to walk in great humility, having a great burden for souls. Our desire is that all men would come to know the One whom we have already experienced.

God began to get our attention through various trials and tribulations and extreme dryness of soul, so that we would return to Bethel with all of our hearts. This we did, crying out to God like Jacob, "I must see you face-to-face."

The Renewal Movement has also been characterized by many notorious sinners and backsliders coming to Christ with a radical commitment and new song of praise in their hearts. The Psalms declare:

> *All you descendants of Jacob, glorify Him.*
> Psalm 22:23

Indeed, the descendants of Jacob are glorifying Him.

The name Jacob means "deceiver," and such were many of those who are coming to the Lord Jesus today, and there is a new and fresh anointing upon the music these former deceivers are writing. It is easy to sense the great gratitude they are expressing for their salvation, because they know, like Jacob knew, that they do not deserve this wonderful grace and love God is pouring out upon His Church.

Many drug addicts and alcoholics are being instantaneously saved and delivered from the grip which Satan has had upon them. Many prostitutes and adulterers and those who have been "hooked" on pornography are

coming to Jesus in this current movement. Sadly, many
of "the religious" have not reached out or loved these
sons of God who have lost their way as they should, so
the Good Shepherd Himself is bringing them back into
the fold. They are understandably so grateful that they
are giving Him their entire beings. Many of these new
converts will go out to the mission fields of the world
and will help to reap the great end-time harvest — just
before the final revealing of the sons of God. Churches
used by God in the Renewal Movement will go out into
the highways and byways and gather in the sinners and
the backsliders whom the religious world has long since
written off.

The Twelve Patriarchs (The Saints' Movement)

God did not stop with Jacob, nor will He stop His work
with the Renewal Movement. Jacob had twelve sons.
While most of them were not models of uprightness,
morality or integrity, yet they became the heads of the
twelve tribes of Israel. I'm so glad God doesn't choose
perfect people to be His sons. The Renewal Movement
will birth sons of God who have not been perfect, and
Jesus will reveal Himself more in and through this group.
This will happen more than either the Church or the
world can imagine at this moment. I am convinced that
these sons are alive today. God will do a quick work in
them to prepare them to help reap His last-day harvest.

Dr. Bill Hamon, one of the most well respected
apostle/prophets alive today, speaks of this restoration
work in the Church: "The Holy Spirit has been commis-

sioned to accelerate His restorational work in the Church. Here is a general overview of what accelerating restoration means: Restorational movements since AD 1500 have accelerated in their frequency of occurrence, from three hundred years apart, to one hundred, to fifty, to every ten years, during the last half of the 20th century. Each prepared the way for the next over the past five hundred years. The Protestant Movement prepared the way for the Holiness Movement and so on: the Pentecostal for the Latter Rain Restoration, for the Charismatic Renewal, for the Faith Movement, for the present Prophetic Movement, which is now preparing the way for the Apostolic Movement, which will, in turn, prepare the way for the Saints' Movement, enabling the saints of the Most High to fulfill Daniel 2:44, 7:18, 22, 27 and Revelation 11:15, 1:5-6 and 5:9-10." [4]

This revealing of the sons of God always begins out of crisis. We are so unlike God, even the best of us, that He must humble us and discipline us, so that we will give Him our undivided attention. This discipline and pruning is never pleasant while we are going through it.

Many of us have already undergone much of the necessary preparation, and we have now come to thank God for every minute of it, because of the revelation of Jesus it has brought to us. At the time we were going through it, however, we thought our world was coming apart. Indeed it was, because our ways are not God's ways nor our thoughts His thoughts. Even so, we had no comprehension of how far our ways were from His ways and our thoughts were from His thoughts. God had to tear our world apart so that we would look to Him and see His world.

Then, God begins to work in us what Paul described in his letter to the Romans:

> *I urge you therefore, brethren, by the mercies of God,*
> *to present your bodies a living and holy sacrifice,*
> *acceptable to God, which is your spiritual service*
> *of worship.*   Romans 12:1

One morning, when I was still half awake and half asleep, Jesus spoke to me about this scripture and the sons of God. He said that if His people would present their bodies, minds and souls to Him, He would walk in their bodies exactly like He did when He was on earth:

> *Truly, truly, I say to you, unless a grain of wheat*
> *falls into the earth and dies, it remains by itself*
> *alone; but if it dies, it bears much fruit. He who*
> *loves his life loses it; and he who hates his life in*
> *this world shall keep it to life eternal.*
>   John 12:24-25

Jesus died, was buried, and was raised on the third day, so that the Church might be born. Through His death and resurrection, He bore much fruit. We, too, must die if we are to bear fruit, for we are to be exactly like Jesus. The Bible is very clear about this:

> *As Thou didst send Me into the world, I also have*
> *sent them into the world.*   John 17:18

Jesus therefore said to them again, "Peace be with you; as the Father has sent Me, I also send you."
John 20:21

Because as He is, so also are we in this world.
1 John 4:17

Jesus, who was God, took on the form of man, that we who are in the form of man might take on the form of God:

He is the image of the invisible God, the first-born of all creation. Colossians 1:15

The world clearly understood there was something very different about Jesus, even if they didn't believe in Him. In this respect, He was the firstborn, and all of us who subsequently have been born again are children as well:

In that day you shall know that I am in My Father, and you in Me, and I in you. John 14:20

Truly, truly, I say to you, he who believes in Me, the works that I do he shall do also; and greater works than these shall he do; because I go to the Father. John 14:12

Jesus knew that after He had conquered Satan, death and the grave, He would pour forth the Holy Spirit. Then, there would be many sons of God, even millions, walking the face of the earth, doing the deeds that He did while He was here. It is up to us now. He completed His work, sat down at the right hand of the Father, and handed the baton to us. In this way, He has given us all authority.

Because we are in the ninth month of pregnancy, we will be revealed to the world in the following ways:

We Will Forgive Sins:

> *If you forgive the sins of any, their sins have been forgiven them; if you retain the sins of any, they have been retained.*   John 20:23

Jesus was not sent to judge the world, but to save the world, and neither are we sent to judge the world. We are sent as ambassadors of Christ, to beg the world to be reconciled to God.

A great anointing of grace to forgive is being poured out on the Church in this last hour. We will have a great compassion for the vilest of sinners, even as Jesus did. He ate with the publicans and sinners, and they enjoyed being with Him. It is even recorded that He ate with Simon the leper, a man who was not even allowed to enter the synagogue. Religious people will not understand when we begin to eat with the lepers of our generation. We dine with the lepers now, so that we may dine with the King later. We forgive the lepers now, so we may be forgiven by the King later, when we all stand before His judgment seat.

Last-day Christians will be extremely cautious about

judging anyone, because they will have a revelation of their salvation beyond that of the Christians of any other generation. They will realize the magnitude of God's love toward them, and therefore they will be able to express this love to the unlovely.

We Will Serve as Jesus Served:

> *Jesus, knowing that the Father had given all things unto His hands, and that He had come forth from God, and was going back to God, rose from supper, and laid aside His garments; and taking a towel, He girded Himself about. Then He poured water into the basin, and began to wash the disciples' feet, and to wipe them with the towel with which He was girded.*   John 13:3-5

Jesus knew that all things had been given unto Him, and that He had come forth from God and was going back to God. We, too, who were chosen before the foundation of the world and are joint heirs with Jesus Christ, are going back to God to rule and reign with our Lord Jesus Christ. Therefore, we can be secure in serving, because we know that God is our Father, and we are joint heirs with our Lord Jesus Christ.

We will have an end-time mindset that enables us to focus on our heavenly reward instead of on our earthly glory. Obviously, we have a long way to go, but God is going to change us very quickly as He reveals Himself to us. When Isaiah saw the Lord and His holiness and

His glory, he was instantaneously changed. When Saul saw Jesus on the road to Damascus, he, too, was transformed immediately. When Jacob wrestled with God, he, also, became a new person. When Moses saw the burning bush, he was transformed.

We see many other examples like these in the Bible, and the one characteristic that all of them have is that their transformation happened immediately. Many of us, like Isaiah, will cry out, *"Woe is me!"* when we see the Lord and realize that ninety percent of what we thought we were doing for Christ has been burned up because we have not been servants, but rather received earthly glory. We have rationalized our selfishness, our prosperity, our pride, our motives and our ambitions, because we were like everyone else. However, when we see our true Example face-to-face, all of our rationalizations are immediately destroyed in the fire of His blazing truth. Then, and then alone, true ministry begins to be birthed.

Suddenly, we will see a world that has become bankrupt spiritually and materially while we have been feasting in a day of famine. As James wrote:

> *You have lived luxuriously on the earth and led a life of wanton pleasure; you have fattened your hearts in a day of slaughter.*   James 5:5

As we cry out, "Woe is me!" we will begin to serve like Jesus served, and the world will take notice.

We Will Walk in Power:

> *But we have this treasure in earthen vessels, that*
> *the surpassing greatness of the POWER may be of*
> *God and not from ourselves.*   2 Corinthians 4:7

> *And He said to me, "My grace is sufficient for you,*
> *for power is perfected in weakness." Most gladly,*
> *therefore, I will rather boast about my weaknesses,*
> *that the POWER of Christ may dwell in me.*
> 2 Corinthians 12:9

God will teach the pregnant ones, by revelation and illumination, of Jacob's secret in the Scriptures. His secret was revealed to the apostle Paul and to many other saints down through the ages, but most Christians today have no comprehension of what it means to walk in brokenness before God. God is about to teach us this lesson. We are about to learn to walk with a continual limp, just as Jacob did.

First, we must wrestle with God, and this is one wrestling match we cannot win. Then we will realize that true power comes from God alone, and we must be as nothing before Him for His power to flow through us. As I have already mentioned, this will give us the power recorded in the book of Acts, because of the revelation that God will give to His last-day sons to equip us to fight the greatest battle of any generation of saints.

Smith Wigglesworth and many others down through the ages learned the secret of power. It is recorded that Wigglesworth raised fourteen people from the dead

during his ministry. Many of us will also raise the dead
in this last-day outpouring. My friend Bob Shattles has
already raised several people from the dead through the
power of Jesus' name.

We Will Be Crucified:

> *I have been crucified with Christ; and it is no longer
> I who live, but Christ lives in me; and the life which
> I now live in the flesh I live by faith in the Son of
> God, who loved me, and delivered Himself up for
> me.*   Galatians 2:20

The first thing we notice about this great mystery of
being *"crucified with Christ"* is that we are not the ones
doing the crucifying. In the same way that God the Father preordained that His Son would be given up and
crucified by the men of His day, God our Father will
also allow circumstances and opposition from the spirit
of the world and principalities and powers in order to
crucify our flesh. Before this Christ Child is revealed,
the opposition we will face and the crucifying process
of our flesh will be greater than at any other time in the
history of the Church. What is required of us is that we
totally surrender our spirits, souls, and bodies to the
purging, purifying and refining process of the Holy
Spirit.

Many of us will not realize what God is doing during
the crucifying process because of the pain we are experiencing. Later, we will thank Him with all of our hearts,
because of the peace, joy and trust this work has

produced in us. We have very little revelation or illumination of the Word of God until He works Galatians 2:20 in us, and being crucified is not a pleasant ordeal!

We Will Abide in Him:

> *I am the true vine, and My Father is the vinedresser. Every branch in Me that does not bear fruit, He takes away; and every branch that bears fruit, He prunes it, that it may bear more fruit. You are already clean because of the Word which I have spoken to you. Abide in Me, and I in you. As the branch cannot bear fruit of itself, unless it abides in the vine, so neither can you, unless you abide in Me. I am the vine, you are the branches; he who abides in Me, and I in him, he bears much fruit; for apart from Me you can do nothing.* John 15:1-5

Two men who lived in previous centuries received from God revelation of this abiding process far beyond their times. One of them was Andrew Murray, who lived in the eighteenth century. The other was Brother Lawrence, who lived in the seventeenth century. I will borrow from the writings of these men to express the abiding process that will take place in today's "ninth-month" Christians.

First, from Andrew Murray's classic, *Abide in Christ:* "Therefore, my brother, who would learn to abide in Jesus, take time each day, ere you read, and while you read, and after you read, to put yourself into living contact with the living Jesus, to yield yourself distinctly and consciously to His blessed influence; so you will give Him the opportunity of taking hold of you, of drawing you up and keeping you safe in His almighty life. He has destined you to something better than a short-lived blessedness, to be enjoyed only in times of special earnestness and prayer, and then to pass away, as you had to return to those duties in which far the greater part of life has to be spent.

"Abiding in Him is not a work that we have to do as the condition for enjoying His salvation, but a consenting to let Him do all for us, and in us and through us. It is a work He does for us — the fruit and the power of His redeeming love. Our part is simply to yield, to trust and to wait for what He has engaged to perform. All His fullness and all His riches are for thee, O believer; for the vine does not live for itself, keeps nothing for itself, but exists only for the branches. The branch does not exist for itself but to bear fruit that can proclaim the excellence of the vine; it has no reason of existence except to be of service to the vine. Abide in Christ!

"This is indeed the Father's object in sending the trial. In the storm, the tree strikes deeper roots in the soil; in the hurricane, the inhabitants of the house abide within, and rejoice in its shelter. It is an unspeakable mercy that the Father comes with His chastisement, makes the world around us all dark and unattractive, leads us to feel more deeply our sinfulness, and for a time, lose our joy in what was becoming so dangerous. He does it in the hope that, when we have found our rest in Christ in time of trouble, we shall learn to choose abiding in Him as our only portion; and when the affliction is removed, have so grown more firmly into Him, that in prosperity He still shall be our only joy. Christian! Pray for grace to see in every trouble, small or great, the Father's finger pointing to Jesus, and saying, 'Abide in Him.' " [5]

The second quote I want to use on this subject is from Brother Lawrence's classic, *The Practice of the Presence of God*: "Ah! knew we but the want we have of the grace and assistance of God, we should never lose sight of Him — no, not for a moment. I know that for the right practice of it, the heart must be empty of all other things, because God will possess the heart alone. Lift up your heart to Him, sometimes even at your meals, and when you are in company; the least little remembrance will always be acceptable to Him. You need not cry very loud; He is nearer to us than we are aware of. One way to recollect the mind easily in the time of prayer, and preserve it more in tranquillity, is not to let it wander too far at other times. Such was my beginning, and yet I must tell you that for the first ten years I suffered much. The apprehension that I was not devoted to God as I wished to be, my past sins always present to my mind, and the great unmerited favors which God did me, were the matter and source of my sufferings." [6]

The world and carnal, backslidden Christians will begin to recognize these "ninth-month" Christians as they learn anew the lesson forgotten in ages past of abiding in Christ and practicing His presence. Indeed, to maintain peace and joy in a world of chaos, this lesson will be learned well, as the Holy Spirit quickens it afresh in the hearts of His pregnant ones.

We Will Become Intimate Friends With Jesus:

> *Greater love has no one than this, that one lay down*
> *his life for his friends. You are My friends, if you*
> *do what I command you. No longer do I call you*
> *slaves, for the slave does not know what his master*
> *is doing; but I have called you friends, for all things*
> *that I have heard from My Father I have made*
> *known to you.*   John 15:13-16

Jesus has been longing for this day. For centuries He has been a friend to His people — in the first trimester, in the second trimester, in the seventh month and in the eighth month — and now, in the ninth month, we will learn to be friends to Him. We will earnestly desire to give Him our best time in the day. We will long to be with Him instead of being friends with the world. We will be honest with Him and share with Him our most intimate thoughts, concerns, joys, successes, failures, fears, anxieties, desires and needs. We will laugh with Him, cry with Him, mourn with Him, rejoice with Him, play with Him, work with Him, dine with Him, rest with Him, vacation with Him, travel with Him and talk with Him every day. We will be concerned about the things He is concerned about. We will love those He loves. We will hate the things He hates. We will gladly suffer with Him when He suffers.

Many of these pregnant ones — regardless of their past sins and failures — will experience the great privilege of seeing Him as Mary Magdalene saw Him after He had risen. Remember, it was not the apostles that He first appeared to. It was to a common sinner who had been forgiven much and therefore loved much. I believe before this birthing process is complete, He will appear to many of His friends. When you begin to be a friend to Jesus, He will reveal the secrets of His heart to you. He can trust you and knows that you will not trample His revelation under your feet.

We Will Have an End-Time Mindset:

> *For our citizenship is in heaven, from which also we eagerly wait for a Savior, the Lord Jesus Christ.*
> Philippians 3:20

> *Set your mind on the things above, not on the things that are on earth.* Colossians 3:2

> *All these died in faith, without receiving the promises, but having seen them and having welcomed them from a distance, and having confessed that they were strangers and exiles on the earth. For those who say such things make it clear that they are seeking a country of their own. And indeed if they had been thinking of that country from which they went out, they would have had opportunity to return. But as it is, they desire a better country, that is a heavenly one. Therefore God is not ashamed to be called their God; for He has prepared a city for them.* Hebrews 11:13-16

These pregnant ones will become heavenly minded. At first, they will not understand what is happening to them because it is all new.

In the last months of a woman's pregnancy, her body chemistry changes, and she has appetites, emotions and intuitions she has never before experienced. She is well aware of the child within her, because she now can feel his kick.

We are also changing. Those who are pregnant with God's Spirit will now feel more at home in His presence in heavenly places, and that is where our minds will abide. We will have such a taste of the heavenly that the earthly will no longer satisfy us. Previously, it was a chore for us to fast and pray, but now we will long to fast and pray so that we may continually experience the heavenly. The Spirit has much work yet to do in us, to change our focus from the temporal to the eternal, but the process is intensifying. Very soon, we will return to the mindset the early believers had.

Frank Bartleman said it well: "Heaven was real to the early Church — far more real than earth. In fact, they seemed to have lived only for the next age. That was their longing, their goal, to be delivered from this present evil world. It was the sole relief they looked forward to. This present life, after all, is the true saint's purgatory. It is the sinner's heaven — his only heaven — and that is sad beyond words to express! But, glory to God, it is our only hell! We are in the enemies' country, running the gauntlet, with foes lined up on all sides — but we're just passing through." [7]

We will be rejected and persecuted. We will share in

His afflictions. We will be ambassadors of Christ. In fact, we will participate in His ministry as prophets, priests and kings. If we truly are sent into the world as He was sent into the world, we will be like Him in every respect. We will participate in His prophetic ministry as a voice of truth to the Church and to the world. We will participate in His priestly ministry as we offer sacrifices of praise, worship and thanksgiving unto God. We will participate in His kingly ministry, as we walk in the authority He delegated to us, to establish His Kingdom upon this earth.

As He leads us into this high calling, the world and its principalities and powers will recognize that sons of God (His pregnant ones) are walking on earth.

Endnotes

1. *Azusa Street*, Frank Bartleman, Whitaker House, New Kensington, PA, 1982, pp. 134, 135, 145.
2. *The Fire That Could Not Die*, Rick Joyner, Morningstar Publications, Charlotte, NC, 1998, p. 37.
3. Ibid. p. 53.
4. *Apostles, Prophets and the Coming Moves of God*, Dr. Bill Hammon, Destiny Image Publishers, Inc., Shippensburg, PA, 1997, p. 19.
5. *Abide in Christ*, Andrew Murray, Christian Literature Crusade, Fort Washington, PA, 1968, pp. 7, 12, 29, 110.
6. *The Practice of the Presence of God*, Brother Lawrence, CBN University Press, Virginia Beach, VA, 1978, p. 30, 38, 41, 42.
7. *Azusa Street*, Frank Bartleman, Whitaker House, New Kensington, PA, 1982, pp. 138-139.

Chapter 5

The Childbirth Classes

And in the same way the Spirit also helps our weaknesses; for we do not know how to pray as we should, but the Spirit Himself intercedes for us with groanings too deep for words; and He who searches the hearts knows what the mind of the Spirit is, because He intercedes for the saints according to the will of God. Romans 8:26-27

As an expectant mother anticipates the delivery of her child, she begins to question herself: "Will I be up to the task? Will I be strong and courageous for the pain of the delivery? Will I know what to do? Will the child be born healthy? Will I know how to care for the child? Will I be able to show love to the child? Will I be a worthy guardian for my child? Will I be selfless enough to sacrifice all for the child?" Such a list could go on and on.

There are some things a mother knows instinctively, but there are many other things for which she needs training. This has led to the establishment of childbirth classes, something that has become, for a great majority of expectant mothers, a normal part of the preparation for the birth. It is the normal culmination of the many months of pregnancy.

Somewhere near the middle of her pregnancy, a mother begins to attend such classes. She arrives with her husband, because he becomes her coach, and there they are surrounded with others who are also pregnant. As the expectant mother looks around the classroom, she sees those who resemble her, and this fellowship with those of like circumstances and goals is comforting.

In the same way, we who are *Pregnant With Christ* resemble each other in the shape of our bodies, the glow on our countenances and our expectant expressions. We enjoy the fellowship of those who are on the same road with us. We will spend a lot of time together during the necessary childbirth classes, and during this time we will develop relationships, some of which will last for a lifetime.

As similar as we all are, we all look a little different, have different personalities, different occupations and different gifts and callings. Our one common bond is the goal of bringing forth the life that is within us.

Probably the most important component of the childbirth class is the instructor, or teacher. The Holy Spirit is the Teacher. The reason we pregnant ones are in the class is that we don't know what to do. We need instruction, so we look to the Teacher to guide us.

The Teacher will begin our instruction by showing us how to rest. It is important that we learn to rest and relax our bodies and minds, in order to learn how to control and overcome the pain associated with childbirth. There are techniques that the Teacher will ask us to learn, practice and make a part of our daily lives.

One of the helpful techniques we will learn is to do

deep-breathing exercises. The Teacher will instruct us on how to reach within ourselves and take the deepest possible breath. This breath will carry us through each contraction when labor comes. The more intense the contraction, the deeper the breath needs to be. This is a very important aspect of the class, because if we do not learn to relax in this way, the pain of childbirth may overwhelm us.

As believers, it is the deep breath of the Holy Spirit that will carry us through the labor pains that will surely come. As we learn to relax, rest and practice our breathing, we will be better prepared to face the approaching task.

In between pains, or contractions, it is important to take the opportunity to relax our bodies. We do not know when the next pain will come, but it definitely will come. We do not know how long the next pain will last, but we want to be ready for it. It is to be expected, and is, in fact, necessary to bring forth the Child.

The next lesson taught by the teacher is the focal point. The focal point is a point of concentration that the mother will choose in the room, or some object she has brought with her to focus on, that will help her to center in, concentrate and remain focused during the labor. This practice of concentration will keep her mind on the task at hand. She will remember the important principles the teacher has given her — if she does not become distracted. If and when a woman becomes distracted, her pain can easily overwhelm her. Therefore, she must always keep her mind focused upon the focal point. As believers, our focal point must always be the Word of God.

The rest, the deep breathing and the focal point are not an end in themselves. They are just tools we pregnant ones will use for the final goal — delivery in the ninth month.

After the preparation for the birth is covered, the teacher will instruct the mother on how to care for her baby. He will teach her how to bathe, feed and handle the child, and how to determine when the baby needs extra care. This will help dispel any anxiety she has been feeling. Knowledge will strengthen her self-confidence and transform her into one who can be trusted with the child. At the conclusion of the childbirth classes, she will be equipped to care for the child. Preparation is the key.

There will be tribulation in bringing forth the child. If we pregnant ones were to go merrily on our way for nine months and not give the birthing process a thought, we would probably be overwhelmed with the first labor pain. Preparation is the key.

If we did not give our health a second thought, and instead ate and drank whatever we pleased, took any kind of medication we pleased, did no exercise, but sat around the house all day, there would be a good chance that we would not be able to bring forth successfully the child within us. Again, preparation is the key.

If we did not learn how to care for the new child upon delivery, we would not be good stewards of one of the greatest gifts God has given us. If we did not pay attention during the classes and focus on the needs of the child, we would not be considered worthy parents. Preparation is the key.

Only the Teacher (Holy Spirit) can train us and convince (convict) us of the necessity to be more concerned about the healthy birth of this child than we are with our own selfish desires. Even as the soon-to-be mother sets aside her lifestyle for the nine-month gestation period, the Holy Spirit now is convicting and convincing many of us to set aside our lives as never before, because we know the birth is near.

It is comforting to find that others in the Body of Christ are sensing this special time and anointing in the earth. While many Christians are going along with their everyday lives as usual, others have this unusual glow on their countenances as they are awaiting the birth. These also have protruding abdomens, full of the Word of God, and they stand out in a crowd. Were it not for their common bond and unique fellowship of the Spirit, they probably could not endure the ostracism from the world and carnal backslidden Christians. These critics are much like those in Noah's day, but the rains did come in his day, and yes, the birth will soon occur as well. It is just as sure.

The Church does not know how to deliver this baby, and therefore must go to childbirth classes. We have never walked this way before, so we must be very dependent upon our Teacher to guide us in this hour:

> *And as for you, the anointing which you received from Him abides in you, and you have no need for anyone to teach you; but as His anointing teaches you about all things, and is true and is not a lie, and just as it has taught you, you abide in Him.*
>
> 1 John 2:27

This does not mean that we are not to listen to the fivefold ministry gifts. It means that we are only to listen to those who are teaching under the influence of the Holy Spirit. Before the true fivefold ministry gifts are in place in the Church, there will be many who claim to be apostles and prophets, but are really only puffed up in their prideful imaginations. We can know the true ministry gifts to the Church by their fruit, humility and power, not by their natural leadership or organizational, administrative and political skills.

As we have said, when a woman is nine months pregnant, she needs plenty of rest. In the same way, we, as pregnant ones, need the rest and teaching provided by the childbirth classes given to us on a daily basis in our prayer closets alone with Jesus. More revelation and illumination of God's Word by the Holy Spirit is coming to the Church in this ninth-month period than we can imagine, but we must come aside and rest to receive the revelation and illumination of the Spirit.

One of the greatest tools of the abortionist (Satan) is keeping us too busy to hear from God. It is time for Christians to turn off or unplug their television sets and computers for certain periods of time and begin to hear the voice of God. In this hour, it is absolutely paramount that we hear from the Holy Spirit. To quote my friend Burt McDaniel: "We must absolutely...

1. Hear His voice, however He speaks.
2. See His glory, however He reveals it.
3. Discern His anointing upon whomever He sends it." [1]

The Holy Spirit has used some very unusual vessels to speak through in the past, and in these last days, He will again astound religious and traditional people by the choice of vessels He uses. He preached to Jonah through a whale and later through a plant; He preached to Peter through a rooster; and He preached to Balaam through a donkey. It is not up to us to question the vessel, but to hear the voice, see the glory and receive the anointing.

I have commented to some that I have learned more about God and experienced more of God in the past two years than in all of the previous twenty-plus years of my walking with Him combined. God revealed so much to the apostle Paul when He took him into the third Heaven that he had to live from then on with a thorn in his flesh to keep him humble. He received so much revelation that he wrote over half the New Testament.

Jesus revealed more of Himself in one sermon to two of His disciples on the road to Emmaus than He did to all of the disciples prior to His resurrection. Jesus revealed His entire end-time plan for the Church in one vision given to the apostle John on the Isle of Patmos.

More revelation and knowledge is being poured out from Heaven right now than in any time in history, but we must come aside to receive it. Begin to expect greater revelation as you have your quiet time with the Lord. Pray Ephesians 1:17-19 and Ephesians 3:14-21. Also, spend much time reading and meditating in the Psalms. This will help you greatly in your preparation for the birth of this Child.

It is extremely important that you learn your breathing techniques to help deliver this baby properly. Nothing should restrict the flow of the breath of the Holy Spirit through you at this late hour of pregnancy. Praying at all times in the Spirit should take on significant new meaning for you. You should try to pray every day in tongues, as well as all throughout the day (in your mind). I have been practicing this for some time, and it is wonderful the amount of edification and strength this brings to my inner man.

As the labor pains increase (and they will increase), we must draw strength, comfort and guidance from the Holy Spirit. This is the hour of the Teacher (Holy Spirit), and we need Him now more than ever. We cannot possibly deliver this child without His help.

Hunger

As part of His work, the Holy Spirit will bring about a hunger in those of us who are *Pregnant With Christ* such as we have never before experienced. There is so much to learn before the birth. A.W. Tozer addressed this unfulfilled hunger fifty years ago, and how much more the need is today: "There is today no lack of Bible teachers to set forth correctly the principles of the doctrines of Christ, but too many of these seem satisfied to teach the fundamentals of the faith year after year, strangely unaware that there is in their ministry no manifest presence, nor anything unusual in their personal lives. They minister constantly to believers who feel within their breast a longing which their teaching simply does not satisfy. I trust I speak in charity, but the lack in our pulpits is real.

Milton's terrible sentence applies to our day as accurately as it did to his: 'The hungry sheep look up and are not fed.'

"The doctrine of justification by faith — a biblical truth, and a blessed relief from sterile legalism and unavailing self-effort — has in our time fallen into evil company and been interpreted by many in such a manner as actually to bar men from the knowledge of God. The whole transaction of religious conversion has been made mechanical and spiritless.

"Every age has its own characteristics. Right now we are in an age of religious complexity. The simplicity which is in Christ is rarely found among us. In its stead are programs, methods, organizations, and a world of nervous activities, which occupy time and attention but can never satisfy the longing of the heart. The shallowness of our inner experience, the hollowness of our worship, and that servile imitation of the world which marks our promotional methods all testify that we, in this day, know God only imperfectly, and the peace of God scarcely at all." [2]

John G. Lake, the great healing evangelist of the early twentieth century, spoke on spiritual hunger in Portland, Oregon, on December 11, 1924. Excerpts from his message are as follows: *"Blessed are they which do hunger and thirst after righteousness, for they shall be filled"* (Matthew 5:6). Hunger is a mighty good thing. It's the greatest persuader I know of. It is a marvelous mover. Nations have learned that you can do most anything with people until they get hungry. But when they get hungry, you want to watch out. There is a certain spirit of desperation that accompanies hunger. I wish we all had it spiritually. I wish to God we were desperately hungry. Wouldn't it be glorious?

"We are sometimes inclined to think of God as mechanical; as though God set a date for this event or that to occur. But my opinion is that one of the works of the Holy Ghost is that of preparer. He comes and prepares the heart of men in advance by putting a strange hunger for that event that has been promised by God until it comes to pass. The more I study history and prophecy, the more I am convinced that when Jesus was born into the world, He was born in answer to a tremendous heart cry on the part of the world. The world needed God desperately. They wanted a manifestation of God tremendously, and Jesus Christ as the deliverer and Savior came in answer to their soul cry.

"The hunger of a man's soul must be satisfied. It must be satisfied. It is a law of God; that law of God is in the depth of the Spirit. God will answer the heart that cries. God will answer the soul that asks.

"William Seymour said, 'Brother, before I met Parham, such a hunger to have more of God was in my heart that I prayed for five hours a day for two and a half years. I got to Los Angeles, and when I got there the hunger was not less but more. I prayed, "God, what can I do?" And the Spirit said, "Pray more." I said, "I am praying five hours a day now." I increased my hours of prayer to seven, and I prayed on for a year and a half more. I prayed God to give me what Parham preached, the real Holy Ghost and fire with tongues and love and power of God like the apostles had.' " [3]

Smith Wigglesworth reportedly had this same hunger and wanted to see it in others. Jack Hywel-Davies wrote of him: "The secret of spiritual success is a hunger that persists. To Wigglesworth the worst that can come to any child of God is to be satisfied with his present spiritual attainments. It is an awful condition, he would tell his hearers. God, he believed, was and is looking for hungry, thirsty people. And that is how Wigglesworth received his baptism." [4]

God will satisfy the hunger of His sheep, the pregnant ones. He is raising up His true fivefold ministers, who themselves are hungry for His manifest presence. Roberts Liardon reported in his book *God's Generals* on two additional great revivalists: "Evan Roberts, the great Welsh revivalist, so hungered after God that God used him to set the world aflame with His Spirit. After receiving his call, Evan wrote to a friend and said, 'I have prayed that the Lord will baptize you and me with the Holy Spirit.' Soon afterward, he got so caught up in the Lord that his bed shook. Then, after that, he was awakened every night at 1:00 am to be 'taken up into divine fellowship.' He would pray for hours, fall back to sleep at 5:00 am for another four hours, then pray from 9:00 am until 12:00 noon. He believed that revival would come through knowledge of the Holy Spirit and that one must 'co-work' with the Spirit in order to operate in power. He carried the ability to usher in the presence of the Holy Spirit as almost a tangible force." [5] Such was his hunger for God!

"Maria Woodworth-Etter, born in 1844, was a hundred years before her time. She lost five of her six children to disease, but this did not hinder her hunger after God.

"Maria had a great vision. Angels came into her room. They took her to the West, over prairies, lakes, forests and rivers, where she saw a long, wide field of waving grain. As the view unfolded, she began to preach and saw the grains begin to fall like sheaves. Then Jesus told her, 'Just as the grain fell, so people [would] fall' as she preached." [6]

In Maria Woodworth-Etter's meetings, people would fall under the power of God and lie for hours, and sometimes days, in the Spirit. Her hunger for God greatly influenced John G. Lake and E.W. Kenyon.

This hunger, brought about by the Holy Spirit in all believers who are *Pregnant With Christ*, is a vital part of bringing about the plan of God in this birthing process.

Appearances

During the childbirth classes, many of the pregnant ones will experience dreams and visions, and many will be privileged to see our Lord before the Birth (the Rapture). In almost every century, He has appeared to a select few, but these appearances will rapidly increase as the time for the birth approaches.

Jesus, of course, appeared to His disciples, but He also appeared to others. In modern times, He appeared to John Alexander Dowie, the great healing apostle. He appeared to Maria Woodworth-Etter, the great healing evangelist. He appeared to John G. Lake, Charles Parham, William Branham, William Seymour and thousands of others.

Smith Wigglesworth was one of those who had this privilege. He said: "I was standing beside her bed looking toward the foot when suddenly the Lord Jesus appeared. I had my eyes opened gazing on Him. There He was at the foot of the bed. He gave me one of those gentle smiles. After a few moments, He vanished. But something that day happened that changed my life. It also changed the whole Clark household. Mrs. Clark was completely healed and lived to raise a family of several children, outliving her husband by several years." [7]

I was at a luncheon once where the guest speaker, Franklin Walden, described how Jesus appeared to him. Franklin is a well-known apostle and prophet of God, especially known in the Southeast. The gentleness in which he described Jesus appearing as a shepherd with a staff in His hand authenticated his experience to me. In an earlier meeting I had requested this meek man of God to lay hands on me. As he did, I physically felt the Holy Spirit as he prophesied that I would be making missionary trips in and out of this country.

One of the great healing evangelists of the Latter Rain Movement, A.A. Allen, was seeking God for His power and described his experience as follows: "So the next day, I was on my knees in the closet again. I had told my wife I would never come out until I heard from God, and I really thought I meant it. But a few hours later, when I began to smell the aroma of food being prepared, I was out of the closet and into the kitchen, inquiring, 'What smells so delicious, Dear?'

"At the table a few moments later, God spoke to my heart. I had only taken one bite of food, when I stopped.

God had spoken to me. I knew in that moment that until I wanted to hear from God more than anything else in the world — more than food and gratification of the flesh — I would never get my answer from God. I quickly rose from the table and said to my wife, 'Honey, I mean business with God this time! I'm going into the closet, and I want you to lock me inside. I'm going to stay there until I hear from God.'

"I had said this so many times before that she was beginning to wonder if I really could subdue the flesh long enough to defeat the devil. 'Oh,' she replied, 'You'll be knocking for me to open the door in an hour or so.' Nevertheless, I heard her lock the door from the outside, saying, 'I'll let you out anytime you knock.' I answered, 'I'll not knock until I have the answer that I've wanted so long.' At last, I had definitely made up my mind to stay there until I had heard from God — no matter what the cost! Hour after hour, I battled the devil and the flesh in that closet! It seemed to me that days were slipping by and progress was so slow. Many times I was tempted to give it all up and try to be satisfied without the answer — to just go on as I had been doing. But deep in my soul I knew I could never be satisfied doing that. I had tried it and found that it was not enough. So I kept on waiting.

"Then the glory of God began to fill the closet. As the interior of the closet began to grow light, I thought my wife had opened the door — but she had not. Jesus had opened the door of Heaven, and the closet was flooded with light. The light of the glory of God! I do not know how long I was in the closet when this happened, and it does not matter. I only know that I prayed *until*! The presence of God was so real and powerful that I felt that I would die right there on my knees. It felt that if God came any closer, I could not stand it. Yet I wanted it and was determined to have it. Was this my answer? Was God going to speak to me? Would He satisfy my longing heart at last after all these years? I seemed to lose consciousness of everything except the mighty presence of God. I tried to see Him and then was afraid that I would, for suddenly I realized that should I see Him, I would die. Just His glorious presence was enough!

"If only He would speak to me now! If He would just answer my question, Lord why can't I heal the sick? Why can't I work miracles in Your name? Why do the signs not follow my ministry, as they did that of Peter, John, and Paul?

"Then, like a whirlwind, I heard His voice! It was God! He was speaking to me! This was the glorious answer that I had been waiting for since my conversion at the age of twenty-three. In His presence, I felt like one of the small pebbles at the foot of the towering Rockies. I felt unworthy to even hear His voice. But He wasn't speaking to me because I was worthy, He was speaking because I was needy. Centuries ago, He had promised to supply that need, and this was the fulfillment of that promise. It seemed that God was talking to me faster than any human could possibly speak — and faster than I could follow mentally. My heart cried out, 'Speak a little more slowly. I want to remember it all.' Yet I knew I could never forget! God was giving me a list of the things that stood between me and His power. After each new requirement was added to the list in my mind, there followed a brief explanation about the requirement and its importance." [8]

In the past, these appearances have been considered to be extraordinary occurrences. We are entering the time when there will be so many appearances of Jesus and His glory that it will no longer be something extraordinary to His pregnant ones. They will see Him in visions and in dreams, while praying and while in reflection. They will also see His glory manifest in various forms. His glory and appearances will be reported in major newspapers and magazines and on television networks. God will allow no one to have an excuse for not receiving Him before He splits the eastern sky.

True Ministers

The Holy Spirit will be a flame of fire that flows through the true ministers of God during these childbirth classes. Smith Wigglesworth declared, "I believe that God's ministers are to be flames of fire. Nothing less than flames, nothing less than mighty instruments, with burning messages, with hearts full of love. They must have a depth of consecration that God has taken full charge of the body and it exists only that it may manifest the glory of God." [9]

Separation

The Holy Spirit will reveal to His pregnant ones during the childbirth classes the separation that will take place. Those who are truly *Pregnant With Christ* already can see this separation that is taking place, but it will intensify in a very short period of time. God does nothing unless He reveals it *"to His servants the prophets"* (Amos 3:7).

Nita Johnson addresses this separating process. An angel appeared to her and stated: "In that day, they will call Him the separator, as He will separate the precious from the vile, the sheep from the goats, and the wheat from the tares.

"The 'precious from the vile' is the truth from the lie. This will facilitate 'the separation of the sheep from the goats.' We will see the sheep and the true shepherds begin to migrate, if you will, toward the pole of this purer truth. Meanwhile, the goats will follow the false shepherds, and together they will make their way to the path leading toward total departure from the truth.

"The third sword of separation will the be the 'wheat from the tares.' That is the Church from the unsaved. The Church will make such a departure from the world system and the ways of the world that it would ordinarily stagger the mind. It won't be difficult by this time to discern who belongs to Christ, that is who, in fact, are the true wheat and who are the tares." [10]

Childlike Dependency

In this birthing process, the Teacher (Holy Spirit) will teach us to be absolutely dependent upon the Father, even as a child is dependent upon his parents:

> *And He called a child to Himself and set him be-*
> *fore them, and said, "Truly I say to you, unless*
> *you are converted and become like children, you*
> *shall not enter the kingdom of heaven."*
>
> Matthew 18:2-3

Only those who are totally dependent upon the Holy Spirit for direction, anointing, wisdom and power will be useful in bringing forth this great birth for which all creation is waiting. We must learn to be totally dependent, like children, if we are to participate in this process.

A Child Is Dependent:

In our world of self-sufficiency, education, careers and pride, we as Christians have a hard time being fully dependent on God. We think we are dependent, but we go through our days making decisions ... without consulting Him. I find that, for me, this comes so naturally I don't even realize I am doing it. After all, I have always been responsible ... to a fault. But a child looks to his parent for everything — for food, safety, comfort, shelter, direction and discipline. How much more should we look to our heavenly Father for all of these.

How many times in the past year have I caught myself being dependent on myself? Now that's a scary thought! Paul said:

> *Indeed, we had the sentence of death within our-*
> *selves in order that we should not trust in ourselves,*
> *but in God who raises the dead.*
>
> 2 Corinthians 1:9

How many times in the past year have I felt the "sentence of death," only to discover I was relying on myself ... again? Becoming dependent on God once again always brought back life and freedom.

A Child Is Trusting:

As children, we did not question the motives and judgments of our parents. We had not been introduced to doubt, fear and the questioning of authority. These are qualities we would acquire from the world and our flesh as we became older. How simple our lives were, as we trusted our caregivers completely. How simple our lives could still be, if, as believers, we could trust our Caregiver in the same manner.

Isaiah said:

> *I will wait for the LORD, who is hiding his face from the house of Jacob. I will put my trust in him.*
> Isaiah 8:17, NIV

Even though there are times that we feel God is hiding His face from us, complete trust brings us peace. Trust is being confident that He is there, whether we see Him or not.

When we were children, we knew that our parents were in our lives. We never questioned it. In the same way, we must never question the presence of our heavenly Father in our lives. We cannot trust our feelings, our intellect, or our flesh in determining His presence in our situation. He always has been, and always will be, in our lives.

A Child Is Carefree:

How we played as children — running, laughing, jumping and singing — without a care in the world! For the most part, we knew we were cared for. For those who did not have this experience as a child, just being childlike can keep a lot of worry at bay. In those days, we had not learned the behavior of our society known as "worry." It is a learned behavior. Instead, we can re-program ourselves to be like the apostle Paul. He said:

> *Be anxious for nothing, but in everything by prayer and supplication with thanksgiving let your requests be made known to God. And the peace of God, which surpasses all comprehension, shall guard your hearts and your minds in Christ Jesus.*
> Philippians 4:6-7

A Child Is Innocent:

When Jesus charged the disciples before sending them out, He said to them:

> *Behold, I send you out as sheep in the midst of wolves; therefore be shrewd as serpents, and innocent as doves.*   Matthew 10:16

What does it mean to be innocent? As a child, we were not yet worldly wise. Innocence was a natural way of thinking for us. It is more difficult to maintain that innocence once we have tasted the world. We are finding that the more we want of God's anointing, the more innocence we must maintain. It seems that daily, weekly and monthly we are called upon to remove something from our lives in order to attain that level of innocence.

Is it worth it? By all means! Obedience is better than sacrifice, especially when sacrificing ultimately leads to more anointing. And only the anointing of the Holy Spirit will facilitate the birthing of this Child.

A Child Is Secure:

> *Those who trust in the LORD are like Mount Zion, which cannot be shaken but endures forever. As the mountains surround Jerusalem, so the LORD surrounds his people both now and forevermore.*
>
> Psalm 125:1-2, NIV

As we learn to trust our parents as children, we will feel secure. We cannot be shaken from this trust. If we place our trust in anything else, our security is shaken. As children, we do not know how to trust ourselves. We have not been schooled by the world to trust our flesh. Self-reliance will come in time, and what an obstacle it will become! But now, as children, we are simply trusting our caregivers, and in that trust we know they want what is best for us.

As we develop a trusting relationship with the Lord, we will find the security we once knew as children. Security in Him will bring us the peace we desire, the place of rest we need and the perseverance to walk the way He desires us to walk, knowing that we cannot be shaken. If we place our trust in anything or anyone else, and our security is based on anything other than our walk with Him, we will find ourselves losing our child-like faith.

A Child Is Expectant:

As children, we expect the best. We look forward to every life experience with the exuberance of a child. We expect every day to be a good one, for we are looking forward to each new adventure. As believers, our expectancy comes in many different facets. In my early years as a believer, I think my expectancy centered around the benefits of being a child of God. I attribute this to a lack of maturity. Not that God doesn't want us to experience His benefits, but as I pressed forward in my mature years, I found that my expectancy was that I would end my race being pleasing to Him.

From his prison cell, the apostle Paul wrote:

> *I eagerly expect and hope that I will in no way be ashamed, but will have sufficient courage so that now as always Christ will be exalted in my body, whether by life or by death.*
>
> Phillipians 1:20, NIV

The older I get, the less I care about what God can do for me. Now, I am more interested in what I can do for Him. It has taken me a long time to get to this place, and I don't want to do anything that would cause me to go backward. If we are to participate with the Holy Spirit in this birthing process, we must be eagerly expecting Jesus to open up new doors of ministry for us.

A Child Is Easily Comforted:

*Blessed are those who mourn, for they will be
comforted.*   Matthew 5:4, NIV

As children, we had many opportunities to be comforted. There were the inevitable "hurts" of life — the scratches, the bumps, the cuts and the broken bones. There were also wounds to the emotions and the spirit, disappointments and griefs. When we experienced these bumps in the road of life, we usually found immediate relief in the arms of a father or mother. Their soft words and gentle arms would quickly restore us to our carefree peace of mind. It is amazing how quickly the pain would disappear when that comfort was afforded.

Shouldn't it be the same way with our heavenly Father? The "bumps in the road" that we experience as believers are perhaps more serious in nature, but the prescription is the same as when we were children. The arms of our heavenly Father are always open wide for our comfort, healing, soothing, reassurance and restoration to security.

Whom do you go to for comfort? I hope you are not one of those who turn to the world for this need. The world can comfort us for a season, but it cannot restore our peace. Peter warmed himself at the wrong fire after he had betrayed Jesus, and it brought no peace. Only when he repented and returned to Jesus did the peace return. Let us never forget who the Source of real comfort is.

A Child Is Well Fed:

Most of us were well fed in our childhoods. We were brought up by nurturing, loving parents, who delighted in offering us the proper foods. Our heavenly Father wants us to be well fed, too, and His Word is all the food we need. The difference, as adults, is that we must *choose* to partake of the food. He has already given it, but we must eat.

The more we feast at the Lord's table and pour His Word into us, the stronger we will grow and the more childlike we will become. We will be able to maintain this childlike relationship if we will feast on His Word on a daily basis. The more we feast, the more dependent, carefree, innocent and expectant we will become. We must continually feast on the Word of God so that the Teacher (the Holy Spirit) can fully train us in the childbirth classes.

Oh, Lord,

May we never outgrow being children in Your presence. May the Holy Spirit thoroughly teach us to walk in childlike dependency, to trust in childlike obedience, to enjoy life with the carefree spirit of a child, to live in childlike innocence, to walk in childlike security, to hope in childlike expectancy, to receive childlike comfort, and to be well-nourished through Your Word, like healthy, well-fed children.
Amen!

When the childbirth classes are completed by our Teacher, the Holy Spirit, we will become mature, walking in the knowledge of the Son of God, attaining to the measure of the stature which belongs to the fullness of Christ, eagerly awaiting the birth of the life within us.

Endnotes

1. *Seize the Day*, Burt McDaniel, Morris Publishing, Keaney, NE, 1996, p. 74.
2. *The Pursuit of God*, A.W. Tozer, Christian Publications, Camp Hill, PA, 1982, 1993, pp. 8, 12, 17.
3. *John G. Lake: The Complete Collection of His Life Teachings*, compiled by Roberts Liardon, Albury Publishing, Tulsa, OK, 1999, pp. 452, 453, 455, 459.
4. *The Life of Smith Wigglesworth*, Jack Hywel-Davies, Vine Books, Servant Publications, Ann Arbor, MI, 1987, by Hodder and Stoughton Limited. First American Edition 1988 by Servant Books, p. 75.
5. *God's Generals*, Roberts Liardon, Albury Publishing, Tulsa, OK, 1996, pp. 82, 85, 89.
6. Ibid. p. 48, 49.
7. *The Life of Smith Wigglesworth*, Jack Hywel-Davies, Vine Books Servant Publications, Ann Arbor, MI, 1987, by Hodder and Stoughton Limited, First American Edition 1988 by Servant Books, p. 53.
8. *God's Guarantee to Heal You*, A.A. Allen, Schambach Revivals, Inc., Tyler, TX, 1991, pp. 178-180.
9. Ibid. p. 74.
10. *Prepare for the Winds of Change II*, Nita Johnson, Eagle's Nest Publishing, Clovis, CA, 1991, pp. 34, 35.

Chapter 6

The Labor Pains

For we know that the whole creation groans and suffers the pains of childbirth together until now. And not only this, but we ourselves, having the first fruits of the Spirit, even we ourselves groan within ourselves, waiting eagerly for our adoption as sons, the redemption of our body. Romans 8:22-23

As the time draws close to the end of the ninth month, a woman will begin to feel the small twinges of discomfort known as "early labor pains." Anytime there is a birth or creation, there is pain involved, and so it is with the birth of a child. The pain of childbirth will usually begin as a tightness around the abdomen. In the beginning, it resembles pressure more than actual pain. The expectant mother then has the sense that a miracle is about to take place.

There is nothing at this point she can do to alter the timing of the miracle, slow it down or keep it from taking place. She is no longer in control of her body. The signs are all there. The goal that she has been preparing herself for is looming before her. She prays that she is ready for the task. She feels as though she is on the crest of a wave and that it is carrying her forward.

As time goes on, the pains begin to come at shorter intervals and with more intensity. The buildup is slow, and she always finds the grace to accept the next threshold of pain. She calls upon her previous training and practice, and uses the tools she has been given by the teacher. She remembers the things He has taught her. As she practices her breathing, taking in deep breaths, she will find the strength to carry herself through each pain.

There are three aspects of spiritual labor pains:

The Push — We push by faith into the glory of God.
The Pull — The Holy Spirit draws us into the glory.
The Pressure — Persecution and tribulation press us into the glory.

The labor pains that I am speaking about here are not those that we think about when speaking of the "Great Tribulation," that seven-year period known to Bible scholars as "the time of Jacob's Trouble."

> Now these are the words which the LORD spoke concerning Israel and concerning Judah;
> "For thus says the LORD,
> 'I have heard a sound of terror,
> Of dread, and there is no peace.
> Ask now, and see,
> If a male can give birth.
> Why do I see every man
> With his hands on his loins, as a woman in childbirth?

And why have all faces turned pale?
Alas! for that day is great,
There is none like it;
And it is the time of JACOB'S DISTRESS,
But he will be saved from it."   Jeremiah 30:4-7

Obviously, these tribulation birth pains will be very severe. The labor pains that carnal and backslidden Christians and unsaved Jews will experience in the Great Tribulation will be very intense indeed. Their groaning and their pain will be significantly greater than the labor pains that we who are caught away in the Rapture will experience. The scriptures that I use here refer to the Great Tribulation, but a portion of this labor will occur before that seven-year period. The pains will begin coming just prior to the Rapture. These are the labor pains we will address. Those Christians who are *Pregnant With Christ* and realize God's appointed hour will not experience the most extreme pains, because they will repent and turn completely to God before the Great Tribulation begins.

Here are some of the warnings offered in the Scriptures of the terrible things that will occur during the period of labor pains:

We have heard the report of it; our hands are limp.
Anguish has seized us, pain as of A WOMAN IN
CHILDBIRTH.   Jeremiah 6:24

And they will be terrified, pains and anguish will
take hold of them; they will writhe like A WOMAN

IN LABOR, they will look at one another in aston-
ishment, their faces aflame.   Isaiah 13:8

As THE PREGNANT WOMAN approaches the
time to give birth, she writhes and cries out in her
LABOR PAINS, thus were we before Thee O LORD.
WE WERE PREGNANT, WE WRITHED IN
LABOR, we gave birth, as it were, only to wind.
We could not accomplish deliverance for the earth
nor were inhabitants of the world born.
                                 Isaiah 26:17-18

But all these things are merely the beginning of
BIRTH PANGS.   Matthew 24:8

For nation will arise against nation, and kingdom
against kingdom; there will be earthquakes in vari-
ous places; there will also be famines. These things
are merely the beginning of BIRTH PANGS.
                                    Mark 13:8

While they are saying, "Peace and safety!" then
destruction will come upon them suddenly like
BIRTH PANGS UPON A WOMAN WITH
CHILD; and they shall not escape.
                              1 Thessalonians 5:3

And they said to him, "Thus says Hezekiah, 'This
day is a day of distress, rebuke, and rejection; for
CHILDREN HAVE COME TO BIRTH, and there
is no strength to deliver.' "   2 Kings 19:3

And a great sign appeared in heaven: A woman
clothed with the sun, and the moon under her feet,
and on her head a crown of twelve stars; AND SHE
WAS WITH CHILD; AND SHE CRIED OUT,
BEING IN LABOR AND IN PAIN TO GIVE
BIRTH. Revelation 12:1-2

Near is the great day of the LORD,
Near and coming very quickly;
Listen, the day of the LORD!
In it the warrior cries out bitterly.
A day of wrath is that day,
A day of trouble and distress,
A day of destruction and desolation,
A day of darkness and gloom,
A day of clouds and thick darkness,
A day of trumpet and battle cry,
Against the fortified cities
And the high corner towers.
And I will bring distress on men,
So that they will walk like the blind,
Because they have sinned against the LORD;
And their blood will be poured out like dust,
And their flesh like dung.
Neither their silver nor their gold
Will be able to deliver them
On the day of the LORD's *wrath;*
And all the earth will be devoured
In the fire of His jealousy,
For He will make a complete end,
Indeed a terrifying one,
Of all the inhabitants of the earth.

Before the decree takes effect —
The day passes like the chaff —
Before the burning anger of the LORD comes upon
you,
Before the day of the LORD's anger comes upon you.
Seek the LORD,
All you humble of the earth
Who have carried out His ordinances;
Seek righteousness, seek humility.
Perhaps you will be hidden
In the day of the LORD's anger.

                              Zephaniah 1:14-18 and 2:2-3

Again, all of these scriptures refer to the Great Tribulation. This will be the most trying time that any man
has ever experienced. Many saints will be born into the
Kingdom during this period. Many Jews will come to
know Jesus as their Messiah during this period. And
many who are now backslidden and have not given their
lives to Christ (and therefore will not be caught up in
the Rapture) will also experience this period.

Those of us who know that we are *Pregnant With
Christ*, however, will also experience pain. It is because
God is growing the Child within us, and He is stretch-
ing us.

Stretch marks will soon appear upon us because we
are being conformed to the image of the Second Adam.
There will be a great transformation in us in the days
ahead. Change does not come without pain.

Again, the worst birth pains will come upon those who
are not *Pregnant With Christ*. Some may have a shallow

relationship with Him, but they have not been impregnated by His Spirit. They are not looking for His return, nor are they living a holy life. They are carnal churchgoers, not disciples. They will experience terrible birth pangs, and the truly pregnant ones will experience only mild birth pangs in comparison.

> *Whenever a woman is in travail she has sorrow, because her hour has come; but when she gives birth to the child, she remembers the anguish no more, for joy that a child has been born into the world.*
>
> John 16:21

The pregnant ones will be able to endure their sorrow. They will travail for the lost, for the evil that is in the world, for the sin in the church, but they will not experience this terrible tribulation. And their sadness will be replaced with great joy as they are caught up with Jesus in the heavens before the Great Tribulation comes. Indeed, when Jesus comes with a shout to receive His Church, these pregnant ones will be reminded of the psalm:

> *For His anger is but for a moment, His favor is for a lifetime; weeping may last for a night, but a shout of joy comes in the morning.*   Psalm 30:5

We must have our wills, our minds and our bodies ready for this birth that will take place, this birth that will be the Rapture of the Church. We are already in labor, and the pains are getting closer and closer together. Finally, there will be one long and constant pain, and then the birth will take place.

Much of the labor pains we will experience will be the result of travailing in prayer, similar to what happened in the Azusa Street Revival. Frank Bartleman records the following: "I found most Christians did not want to take on a burden of prayer. It was too hard on the flesh. I was carrying this burden now in ever-increasing volume, night and day. My life was, by this time, literally swallowed up in prayer. I was praying day and night. At Smaley's church one day, I was groaning in prayer at the altar. The Spirit of intercession was upon me. A brother rebuked me severely. He did not understand it. The flesh naturally shrinks from such ordeals. The 'groans' are no more popular in most churches than is a woman in birth pangs in the home.

"Soul travail does not make pleasant company for selfish worldings, but we cannot have souls born without it. Childbearing is anything but a popular exercise, and so with the real revival of newborn souls in the churches. Men run from the groans of a woman in travail of birth. And so the church desires no 'groans' today. She is too busy enjoying herself." [1]

And so it is with the twenty-first-century Church today. Much of the Church is too busy enjoying the blessings and comforts of Christ to participate in the afflictions and sufferings of Christ (soul travail and groanings that birth souls into the Kingdom).

In the days to come, we will have persecution from within and without. Those who may have a very shallow relationship and those who are backslidden will not understand our fervency during this last hour just prior to the Rapture. So we will be persecuted from within. And we'll certainly be persecuted from without, because the world does not understand what is going on. We'll be misunderstood and rejected by Christians as well as unbelievers.

We'll experience some very bizarre happenings and occurrences even before the Rapture occurs. Satan will begin to exhibit his limited power, and his evil deeds will become more apparent. He was a murderer from the beginning, and his acts of terror and evil will become evident to all during these last days.

In response, God will raise up a standard with far greater power. The pregnant ones will see the glory of God. This glory will appear in manifest form.

These victorious pregnant ones who compose the end-time Church will very soon depart as a victorious, glorious Church, and will escape the Great Tribulation (Jacob's Trouble) coming upon planet Earth.

Many of these pregnant ones will receive mountain-top experiences to help them endure their labor pains. Smith Wigglesworth describes one of these experiences: "One day in the early nineteen hundreds, I went to the top of a high mountain in Wales for a time of prayer. The Lord's presence seemed to envelop and saturate me, reminding me of the transfiguration scene. I was impressed with the thought that the Lord's only purpose in giving us such glorious experiences is to prepare us for greater usefulness in the valley." [2]

Comparisons With the Invasion of Normandy

Right now, I believe the Church is experiencing labor pains similar to the pain the Allies experienced when they invaded Normandy during World War II. Much preparation, coordination and training preceded the invasion. Even so, no amount of preparation could ready the individual soldier for the hell he would experience as he landed on those beaches. No amount of coordination could have anticipated the fierce assault of the enemy, the sudden change of weather, and the inevitable weakness of human error. No amount of training could prepare those brave men for the loss of their best friends as their bodies were torn asunder by the weapons of the enemy.

In the same way, the Church has had two thousand years to prepare for the events that will soon take place. However, much of that time was spent in the Dark Ages, and truths lost in those years are just now being restored to the Church.

Sadly, many denominations and their leadership have actually only allowed one major doctrine to be restored to its fullness — justification by faith. Other segments of the Church emphasize certain other doctrines that have been restored, while totally neglecting other equally important doctrines. Very few churches are indeed walking in all the doctrines of the first-century Church. These include justification by faith, water baptism, the baptism of the Holy Spirit, sanctification, the gifts of the Holy Spirit, the fivefold ministry gifts to the Church, the authority of the believer, divine healing and deliverance from demonic powers.

Meanwhile, the enemy has built up heavily fortified bunkers of division, tradition, immorality, cultural mindset, worldliness, pride, fear, etc. All of these must be destroyed, and that is not an easy task. It will not be accomplished without great pain and sacrifice.

Like the Nazis, the enemy knows the invasion is coming. He just isn't sure about the date. I believe the last invasion has already begun. God's army, however, like the Allies at Normandy, is stranded on the beach. Also similar to the experience of the Allies at Normandy, the Church is experiencing heavy losses because the enemy is in heavily fortified positions on higher ground.

The Allies knew they must get off the beach, destroy the enemy bunkers and eventually take Berlin, but their losses were heavy because they were stranded. They had not anticipated all the minefields, the constant mortar fire, the embedded machine-gun fire, the Panzer tank divisions, the high rate of casualties, the miscalculations on parachute drops, the death of much of the leadership, the psychological trauma of the conflict, the noise, the stench, the desertions, the deaths by friendly fire, the sheer terror, the battle fatigue and the paralysis of fear that many experienced, the taunting voice in their minds saying, "You will be defeated and die on this beach" — and, most of all, the utter confusion.

The abortionist (Satan) knows that if he can keep the Church stranded on the beach, he can stop the invasion, which has already begun. He has been successful previously, using a variety of tactics. They have included persecution, worldliness, false doctrines, lukewarmness and even prosperity.

Now, however, much more is at stake, and he knows it. Once the Church gets off the beach, she will enter into the heart of the enemy's camp. The harvest will be reaped and in spite of the labor pains, the Birth (Rapture) will take place. Such are the stakes of this invasion. It is no great surprise that the Church is already experiencing mild labor pains. The most severe pains will come later, after the pregnant ones have departed.

It is not difficult to see the symbolism involved in the invasion of Normandy versus the unseen invasion by the Church of the domain of darkness. Remember, Jesus said:

> *And from the days of John the Baptist until now, the kingdom of heaven suffers violence, and violent men take it by force.*   Matthew 11:12

Labor pains occur when unsuspecting, naive Christians are killed or wounded by hidden minefields (the craftily concealed deceptions of the enemy). One of the greatest deceptions in this country is that we can take the Kingdom through marketing the Gospel without the power of the Holy Spirit, totally ignoring Paul's warning:

> *For the kingdom of God does not consist in words but in power.*   1 Corinthians 4:20

The Word of God is the weapon that will defeat the deceptions of the enemy (his hidden minefields). Many Christians who lack perseverance will be killed or wounded by the constant, consistent mortar fire of the enemy.

Another great weapon of the enemy is his consistent temptation aimed at our weaknesses. After tempting Jesus in the wilderness, he left Him, but only to wait for a more opportune time. Satan doesn't fight fair. He knows what lines of our defenses are weak, and attacks us at our weakest moment. Perseverance is the weapon that will defeat the consistent temptations the enemy sends our way.

Other Christians, who are not as strong as those wounded by mortar fire, will be wounded and killed by embedded machine-gun fire (the little foxes that spoil the grapes). These include the lack of discipline of the appetites, and especially the lack of discipline of the tongue. Discipline is the weapon that will defeat the little foxes that spoil the grapes, our fleshly appetites, etc.

Some strong Christians will be taken out by the Panzer tank divisions. Like the Nazis, these Christians also have tanks, but they are no match for the Panzers. These Christians are strong, but have forgotten the admonition: *"Therefore let him who thinks he stands take heed lest he fall"* (1 Corinthians 10:12). Self-confidence will be their demise. We are fighting a worthy adversary. He is stronger than we are, but he is not stronger than He who is within us. Humility is the weapon that will defeat self-confidence.

Still other Christians will fall when they take their eyes off their Commander In Chief, and look at the wounded and dead falling all around them. Men's hearts will fail them for fear of what is coming upon the earth. Courage is the weapon that will defeat the enemy when a close friend is wounded or killed in battle.

Even as the Allies made serious miscalculations in their parachute drops, some Christians will miscalculate the domain of the enemy and fall right into his trap. For instance, they will not guard their eyes from the flood of pornography invading our computers and televisions. Discernment is the weapon that will defeat fleshly miscalculations encouraged by the enemy.

Many Christians will be disillusioned, with the death of the old guard of leadership and the fall of other leadership into false doctrine and immorality. Trust in the Commander In Chief is the weapon that will defeat disillusionment when other leadership fails us.

As with the Allies, the psychological trauma of the conflict will take its toll on not a few, and they will turn to psychologists and tranquilizers rather than the Holy Spirit. The peace of God is the weapon that will defeat the psychological trauma of the enemy.

The noise from the mines exploding, the tank fire, the heavy gunfire from the ships, the grenades bursting, the mortar fire and the machine-gun fire was deafening to the Allies and brought them into a state of numbness. The constant barrage of fiery missiles from the enemy into the Christian's mind numbs him so he will remain on the beach of mediocrity and unbelief. The shield of faith is the weapon that will defeat fiery missiles and noises that are distractions from the enemy.

The stench of the dead bodies combined with the stench of the gunpowder and blood upon the beach was nauseating to the Allies. The stench of Christians walking in the flesh, far below their calling, must be nauseating to God. While He is urging them to get off the beach and take the land, many will choose to walk in their lower nature, while making the excuse "We are only human." The fragrance of the Holy Spirit, as we abide in Him and walk in Him, is the weapon that will defeat the stench of our flesh.

The deserters that fateful day in Normandy were few in number, but other brave men were weakened and tempted to follow them from the heat of the conflict. In the same way, weaker brethren, who have no stomach for warfare — who only enjoy sitting in church services — will be a discouragement to those who are sacrificing everything to take the land and bring about the birth of this Child. Praise is the weapon that will defeat discouragement and cause us to stand firm and not desert our mission.

One of the most horrible tragedies of the conflict with Nazi Germany at Normandy was the death of many Allies by friendly fire. This discouraged everyone, and to those who carelessly or accidentally fired the shots, the grief, guilt and shame was overwhelming. As the Church is stranded on the beach, many Christians are very careless with their tongues and are used to destroy and weaken other Christians. Some even take it upon themselves to finish off Christians whom the enemy has already wounded. Others accidentally wound their fellow soldiers because they are so caught up in their own ministries that they forget that their ministries are only a small part of the army, and they trample underfoot other believers whose gifts are equally important in getting the army off the beach. Love is the weapon that will esteem others more highly than ourselves and keep us from wounding our brothers and sisters with "friendly fire."

The sheer terror the Allied soldiers experienced that day at Normandy was overwhelming, even to the most seasoned veteran. While the Church is struggling to get off the beach, even the strongest of Christians experience days when they begin to wonder, "Are we ever going to take the land?" God's presence is the weapon that will defeat sheer terror in the midst of battle.

Battle fatigue began to affect many at Normandy, especially those who were older, improperly trained and out of shape. Those Christians who are not fully equipped with the weapons of their warfare and are not disciplined will be of no use in this battle. They will quickly faint in the day of adversity and will only be a burden to stronger Christians. The joy of the Lord is the weapon that will defeat battle fatigue in a long skirmish.

Some soldiers were so paralyzed by fear at Normandy that they could not even discharge their weapons. Fear is a terrible weapon in the hands of the enemy. It must be destroyed by faith. The abortionist (Satan) is well aware of the value of his mighty weapon of fear, and he will paralyze Christians who are walking in unbelief with this weapon. Faith is the weapon that will destroy the paralysis caused by fear.

The voice many Allied soldiers heard in their minds that day at Normandy was "You will be defeated and die on this beach." Many Christians will hear this same voice in the middle of the conflict, but this is not the greatest weapon of the enemy in the area of the mind. C.S. Lewis describes it best in his classic, *The Screwtape*

Letters. In the book the seasoned, older devil, Screwtape, is speaking to his understudy, Wormwood, and he says, "It is funny how mortals always picture us as putting things into their minds. In reality, our best work is done by keeping things out." [3] The most devastating work the enemy will do in the coming days in the minds of the believers is to prevent us from hearing the voice of the Holy Spirit, "Victory is at hand." The Holy Spirit is the weapon that will speak comforting truth to our minds and shield out all other voices.

The utter confusion of the conflict at Normandy disabled the allied army, as platoons were destroyed and scattered on the beach. One of the main reasons the Church has not made further progress in its invasion is that there is no clear sound of the trumpet to the broader Church. In most arenas, every wind of doctrine prevails. Only a small remnant of people have paid the price and right now are clearly hearing the voice of the Commander In Chief, the Lord Jesus Christ.

The prophetic voice is not being heard by the larger part of the Body of Christ in this hour. In the near future, prophetic voices, like John the Baptist's, will rise out of total obscurity and bring clear direction to the Church. A prophetic voice is the weapon that will remove the utter confusion by saying, "This is the way, walk ye in it."

There's one major difference between the Allied invasion of Normandy and the Church's invasion of spiritual Normandy. The Allies had a great sense of purpose against the evil Nazi regime and understood that it would take a total unified effort to defeat their common enemy. The Church has not yet understood that we cannot get off the beach until we come into unity. There-fore, division and disharmony, primarily as a result of impure motives and selfish ambition, is keeping the Church on the beach.

The bottom line is — we are not walking in enough love. Paul declared:

> *And beyond all these things put on love, which is*
> *the perfect bond of unity.*   Colossians 3:14

When all else fails, we must return to the Word of God for direction. Here, the Word tells us clearly that a lack of love is the cause for our divisions. Love is *"the perfect bond of unity."* When we learn to lay down our lives for the good of the whole, as Jesus did, we will march eas-ily through the land and take the enemy territory. Yes, there will be labor pains, as long as we are stranded on the beach. But, things are about to change, and we will take our spiritual Berlins.

The Allies had excellent leadership in General Dwight "Ike" Eisenhower, General Omar Bradley, General George Patton and others. However, these men cannot be spoken of in the same breath with our Commander in Chief, the Lord Jesus Christ. He will lead us to vic-tory by the power of the Spirit, and this baby will be birthed, and our ultimate war will be won.

Much of the leadership of the allied assault was de-stroyed before the troops got off the beach. Then, literally overnight, privates became sergeants, sergeants became captains and captains became colonels. Scattered, dis-abled platoons were pieced together, and natural leaders with little experience rose up to lead the platoons. They had one goal — to get their soldiers off of the beach. Innovative strategies, not planned in advance, had to be initiated. Brave men, with great courage, would pick up a flame-thrower, not even knowing how to use it. Radical attacks against the embedded bunkers cost many their lives, but in the end, they did get off the beach. With this ragtag group of new leaders, exhausted, yet still marching, the Allied troops made their way into France and onward to Berlin.

So, how is the Church going to get off the beach? Not without pain. Not without losses. Not without innovative ideas. Not without a change in leadership. Not without the flame-thrower of the fire of God. Not without persecution. Even now, our Commander in Chief has raised up a bold, new type of leadership. Many young preachers, in their late twenties, early thirties and early forties, have been called upon to get the Church off the beach. The churches led by these men and women have quickly grown from a few hundred to several thousand, and those who are not tripped up by pride will continue to grow.

For many reasons, these new leaders were not God's first choice. It may have been because of their lack of experience, a questionable theology, a sensational approach or their general youthfulness. Still, Jesus had to use someone, and old wineskins wouldn't do.

Many of these emerging leaders are women, and they are stepping forward to fulfill their own God-given destinies in leadership. At some point, the gray-haired generation will hopefully understand more fully what God is doing and join the battle. Right now, many of the baby boomers are living in a past move of God. For this reason, God has resorted to the baby busters. The churches led by this new group of men and women have several things in common: radical faith, radical power, radical praise and worship and radical evangelism. Soon, God will begin to challenge them to move into radical discipleship and death to self. The Church cannot get off the beach without this.

Burt McDaniel speaks to the new leadership in his book *Seize the Day*: "Regardless of your education, training, position, or lack thereof, you will not be automatically ushered into anything with God. Your job service record will not qualify you for any exemptions of the requirements. I'm sure many of you who read these words have impressive resumes in God, but hear me, 'It's time for recertification.'

"God is not in the business of casting away what He has established in order to move on. At times, God does seem to neglect established order and move to other leadership in order to advance. This does not happen because this is His chosen way of operating. He moves to new people because His established flock has grown dull of hearing, or has become stagnated in its present position, or has lost the driving desire to cooperate with the next plan of action.

"He has invested heavily in His present leadership and desires to use them. However, He is fully capable of raising up a 'new nation that will produce the correct fruit of His kingdom for that time.' Therefore, we are not necessarily talking about new leadership, but, hopefully, established leadership that will catch a fresh vision of His purposes for our time.

"I do understand He is bringing forth what appears

to be new leaders into places of prominence. Many of these will not actually be new, but like Moses, they will be found walking out of the desert places of preparation. There they have met God and themselves. They now come forth refined and with a singular mission. There will be new leaders, but they will come alongside many who have had their swords sharpened, and are preparing to reengage the battle with a greater degree of understanding." [4]

While old wineskins and traditional churchgoers are trying to determine which new church program will cause growth, generation X'ers are swimming, diving, jumping, belly-flopping, dog-paddling and floating in the river of Holy Ghost revival that is beginning to sweep this nation. Many young people are coming to altars weeping radical tears of repentance, expressing wonderful laughter of joy, giving great shouts of victory and falling under the awesome hand of God.

This generation is desperate for the supernatural. They have sought it in drugs, sex and the occult. Having been disillusioned and deceived, they are now experiencing a "high without a hangover," an "experience without entrapment" and "pleasure without penalty." They have found the words of Jesus to be true: *"If any man is thirsty, let him come to Me and drink. He who believes in Me, as the Scripture said, 'From his innermost being shall flow rivers of living water' "* (John 7:37-38). The challenge to the Church is to unstop the wells, let the river flow, get off the beach and take the land.

The overcomers will be the true pregnant ones who overcome the pain of childbirth, take the Kingdom of God by force, march to spiritual Berlin and prepare the

Church for the Birth (the Rapture). The Spirit of the Lord
has much to say about these overcomers in John's
Revelation:

> *He who has an ear, let him hear what the Spirit*
> *says to the churches. To him who overcomes, I will*
> *grant to eat of the tree of life, which is in the Para-*
> *dise of God.*   Revelation 2:7

> *He who has an ear, let him hear what the Spirit*
> *says to the churches. He who overcomes shall not*
> *be hurt by the second death.*   Revelation 2:11

> *He who has an ear, let him hear what the Spirit*
> *says to the churches. To him who overcomes, to him*
> *I will give some of the hidden manna, and I will*
> *give him a white stone, and a new name written on*
> *the stone which no one knows but he who receives*
> *it.*   Revelation 2:17

> *AND HE WHO OVERCOMES, and he who keeps*
> *My deeds until the end, to him I will give author-*
> *ity over the nations.*   Revelation 2:26

> *HE WHO OVERCOMES shall thus be clothed in*
> *white garments; and I will not erase his name from*
> *the book of life, and I will confess his name before*
> *My Father, and before His angels.*
>   Revelation 3:5

> *HE WHO OVERCOMES, I will make him a pil-*
> *lar in the temple of My God, and he will not go out*

from it anymore; and I will write upon him the name of My God, and the name of the city of My God, the new Jerusalem, which comes down out of heaven from My God, and My new name.

Revelation 3:12

HE WHO OVERCOMES, I will grant to him to sit down with Me on My throne, as I also overcame and sat down with My Father on His throne.

Revelation 3:21

HE WHO OVERCOMES shall inherit these things, and I will be his God, and he will be My son. Revelation 21:7

These pregnant ones are the overcomers. They will not only overcome labor pains; they will overcome trials and tribulations, afflictions and temptations, and persecutions and distresses. They are now ready to receive their reward.

Yes, we are experiencing some mild labor pains right now on the beach, but it is time to hear the voice of the Commander in Chief, because victory is at hand!

Endnotes

1. *Azusa Street*, Frank Bartleman, Whitaker House, New Kensington, PA, 1982, pp. 14, 15, 23, 24.
2. *The Life of Smith Wigglesworth*, Jack Hywel-Davies, Servant Publications, Ann Arbor, MI, 1987, p. 80.
3. *The Screwtape Letters*, C.S. Lewis, Lord and King Associates. Inc., West Chicago, IL, 1976, p. 34.
4. *Seize the Day*, Burt McDaniel, Morris Publishing, Kearney, NE, 1996, pp. 37, 118, 119.

Chapter 7

The Physician

Can a woman forget her nursing child, and have no compassion on the son of her womb? Even these may forget, but I will not forget you.

Isaiah 49:15

God is the Physician, and He will deliver this Baby in perfect health. This will be a natural childbirth; no drugs will be used. There will be nothing unnatural or counterfeit about it in any way.

There have been many false labors and aborted births, but the Great Physician will ensure that this Child is born in perfect health, without spot or wrinkle. False physicians and old midwives have many times hindered the birth of this Child, but the Great Physician was always there, waiting for the proper time, the fullness of time, when the Child would come forth.

A woman must have total confidence in her physician. If she does not, she will be unsure of his ability to see her through the task ahead. She will be unsure of every instruction she receives from him. That is why it is important that she have confidence in his ability to see her through.

The Church and individual members will develop great trust in the Great Physician in this last hour. God, the Physician, will deliver this Baby when there is absolute trust in His ability. A group of the pregnant ones will have such a great trust in God that their confidence in His power and protection will be an example to the larger part of the Body of Christ. God has longed for a people who would trust Him, and time and time again He has been disappointed. This is changing even now, since God has put many of His pregnant ones through the furnace of affliction, and they found that He was in the fire with them.

Trust comes only through extreme trials. Peter knew this and wrote about it:

> *In this you greatly rejoice, even though now for a little while, if necessary, you have been distressed by various trials, that the proof of your faith, being more precious than gold which is perishable, even though tested by fire, may be found to result in praise and glory and honor at the revelation of Jesus Christ.* 1 Peter 1:6-7

> *Beloved, do not be surprised at the fiery ordeal among you, which comes upon you for your testing, as though some strange thing were happening to you.* 1 Peter 4:12

Peter was very confident of his faith level in the Great Physician until he denied Christ three times. Afterwards, he experienced the furnace of affliction, which burned up all of his self-confidence so that he could learn to trust God and not himself. There will be many like Peter, in this last hour, who will find that their faith has not been tried. They will realize they were leaning on the deception of self-confidence, thinking they were trusting God, until God burned up all of their self-confidence, self-effort and selfish ambition with the blaze of His fire.

Isaiah also learned to trust God after he walked through the fire:

> *When you pass through the waters, I will be with you; and through the rivers, they will not overflow you. When you walk through the fire, you will not be scorched, nor will the flame burn you.*
>
> Isaiah 43:2

> *Behold, I have refined you, but not as silver; I have tested you in the furnace of affliction.*
>
> Isaiah 48:10

Isaiah came from an aristocratic family. He was very well educated, and he socialized with the upper crust of society. He rubbed shoulders with royalty. He gave advice to leaders of nations. Because of all these factors, Isaiah trusted his intellect, his blue-blood upbringing and his social contacts, until one day he saw the Lord and cried out:

> *Woe is me, for I am ruined! Because I am a man of unclean lips, and I live among a people of unclean lips; for my eyes have seen the King, the LORD of hosts.*   Isaiah 6:5

From that point on, Isaiah trusted the Great Physician.

Many aristocratic Christians, like Isaiah, will realize their education, blue-blood upbringing and social contacts are of no value to them when they stand before a holy God. Like Isaiah, they will also say, *"Woe is me, for I am ruined!"* Then they will begin to trust in the Great Physician.

Abraham, the father of our faith, was tried severely, so that he could become an example to us in these last days. Like Jesus, he learned obedience through the things he suffered. His great trust in offering Isaac, his only begotten son, is the trust God is saying He desires from us today. In the coming days, God will raise up sons of Abraham, heirs according to promise, and they will trust the Physician as no other generation has.

Many of you are going through the valley experience in your life right now. God is simply working true trust into your life. This is one of the most difficult lessons that pregnant ones must learn.

Joseph was a "golden-haired" boy who became enamored of the favor he had with God and the wonderful revelations he had received from God. He had no idea that to those to whom God gives great favor and great revelation, He also gives great affliction and tribulation. Just ask Paul!

Like many pregnant ones in this hour, Joseph had to be taught that favor and revelation are through God's grace, not through golden hair. After being put through the furnace of affliction, favor and revelation are not so important anymore — only the faithfulness of the Great Physician. In the last days, these pregnant ones will gladly lay down their favor, gifts and revelation as crowns before the feet of Jesus. All they will care about is abiding in His presence.

There will be many reluctant prophets like Jonah who will be taught that trust and obedience are better than swimming with the fishes. Others, like Job, will be taught that God is just in all His dealings, even though at times we cannot see His justice because of the severity of the trial and the weakness of our flesh. Still others, like David, will be taught that God is faithful — even when we are faithless. Whatever Bible character we examine, whatever story we read, one thing remains the same: God will have a group of pregnant ones who will completely trust Him in these last days.

The Physician (God the Father) will cause the Bride to trust Him with a powerful demonstration of His fire upon His people. Much is spoken of concerning the fire of God in this hour. Many churches are having Friday night fires. Others speak of revival fire. The fire of God fell upon the Church on the Day of Pentecost fifty days following the resurrection. On that day, God's commandments were written by the Spirit on the hearts of believers. Three thousand were saved on that day. The world did not understand what occurred that day. Neither do they understand today:

> *And when the day of Pentecost had come, they were all together in one place. And suddenly, there came from heaven a noise like a violent, rushing wind and it filled the whole house where they were sitting. And there appeared to them tongues as FIRE*

*distributing themselves, and they rested on each one
of them. And they were all filled with the Holy Spirit
and began to speak with other tongues, as the Spirit
was giving them utterance.*　　　　Acts 2:1-4

This is when the fire of God fell upon the believers in
the first century, but God's people have always known
that He was the God of fire and that they could trust
Him. The writer of Hebrews describes the first Pentecost when the Law was given from Mount Sinai. This
occurred fifty days after the crossing of the Red Sea. The
commandments of God were written by the finger of
God on tablets of stone. Three thousand were slain on
that day:

*For you have not come to a mountain that may be
touched and to a blazing fire, and to darkness and
gloom, and whirlwind, and to the blast of a trumpet and the sound of words which sound was such
that those who heard begged that no further word
should be spoken to them. For they could not bear
the command, "If even a beast touches the mountain, it will be stoned." And so terrible was the
sight, that Moses said, "I am full of fear and trembling." But you have come to Mount Zion and to
the city of the living God, the heavenly Jerusalem,
and to myriads of angels, to the general assembly
and church of the first-born who are enrolled in
heaven, and to God, the Judge of all, and to the spirits of righteous men made perfect, and to Jesus, the*

mediator of a new covenant, and to the sprinkled blood, which speaks better than the blood of Abel.

See to it that you do not refuse Him who is speaking. For if those did not escape when they refused Him who warned them on earth, much less shall we escape who turn away from Him who warns from heaven.

And His voice shook the earth then, but now He has promised, saying, "Yet once more I will shake not only the earth, but also the heaven." And this expression, "Yet once more," denotes the removing of those things which can be shaken, as of created things, in order that those things which cannot be shaken may remain. Therefore, since we receive a kingdom which cannot be shaken, let us show gratitude, by which we may offer to God an acceptable service with reverence and awe; FOR OUR GOD IS A CONSUMING FIRE.   Hebrews 12:18-29

In the book *The Midrash Says*, by Rabbi Moshe Weissman, the author wrote: "On the occasion of Matan Torah (the giving of the Torah), the Bnai Yisrael (Children of Israel) not only heard Hashashem's (the L_rd's) voice but actually saw the sound waves as they emerged from Hashashem's (the L_rd's) mouth. They visualized them as a fiery substance. Each commandment that left Hashashem's (the L_rd's) mouth traveled around the entire camp and then to each Jew individually, asking him, "Do you accept upon yourself this commandment with all the halochot (Jewish law) pertaining to it?" [1]

God Has Always Revealed Himself as a Consuming Fire

The Physician (God the Father) has always revealed Himself as a consuming fire. He revealed Himself to Moses in the burning bush. Moses later found that there was healing and unimaginable power in this fire. He revealed Himself to the children of Israel as a pillar of fire at night, giving direction and protection wherever they went. He revealed Himself to Isaiah in the coals of fire that cleansed the prophet's lips. He spoke to Jeremiah, *"Is not My word like fire?"* (Jeremiah 23:29). Ezekiel described God looking like fire on His throne, *"from His loins upward."* Daniel saw His throne ablaze with flames, its wheels a burning fire. A river of fire was flowing and coming out from before Him (see Daniel 7:9-10).

The apostle Paul said, *"The Lord Jesus shall be revealed from heaven ... in flaming fire, dealing out retribution to those who do not know God and to those who do not obey the gospel of our Lord Jesus."* (2 Thessalonians 1:7). John the Revelator described the Lord's eyes as being *"like a flame of fire."* The writer of Hebrews described Him as *"a consuming fire."*

God has always revealed Himself as a consuming fire. He wants His people to know that He can be trusted. He is the Physician and will deliver this Child in perfect health.

The Fire of God Destroys His Enemies

Those who are *Pregnant With Christ* can fully put their confidence in and trust the Physician (God the Father)

because He will destroy with fire all who oppose this
Christ Child being born. Nadab and Abihu offered
strange fire before the Lord and lost their lives because
of it:

> *Now Nadab and Abihu, the sons of Aaron, took
> their respective firepans, and after putting fire in
> them, placed incense on it and offered strange fire
> before the* LORD, *which He had not commanded
> them. And fire came out from the presence of the*
> LORD *and consumed them, and they died before the*
> LORD.   Leviticus 10:1-2

Many unbelievers today are caught up in the occult
and are offering strange fire before the Lord through
witchcraft, astrology, palm reading, psychic interpreta-
tions, tarot cards and ouïja boards. Others, including
many Christians, are offering up the strange fire of lust,
pornography, marijuana, cocaine, alcohol, nicotine, etc.
Not to be outdone, many ecclesiastical churches are offering up the strange fire of respectability, tradition,
cultural Christianity, oratory, unbelief, charm and charisma, religious philosophy, professionalism, legalism,
sensationalism, etc. Far too little true anointed worship
is being offered up to God.

All of us have offered up strange fire to God at one
time or another in our lives. Except for His grace and
love, we would all be destroyed like Nadab and Abihu.
So many, both Christians and unbelievers, are addicted
to the strange fire they are offering that the very thing
they are offering has become their bondage.

Robert Palmer wrote a song that included the lyrics, "Might as well face it — I'm addicted to love." The world sings this song and really means, "I'm addicted to lust." Unbelievers (and also many believers) are addicted to all manner of strange fire in their search for the true fire that will satisfy them. There is only one addiction that is not self-destructive, and this is the only real cure for all other self-destructive addictions. It is being addicted to the anointing of God.

Nadab and Abihu were not the only ones with whom the Lord was angry. When the children of Israel murmured against Moses, the Lord consumed some of them with fire. Isaiah said, *"Fire will devour Thine enemies"* (Isaiah 26:11). Lucifer once walked in the midst of stones of fire until unrighteousness was found in him, but in the end, the fire will consume him (see Ezekiel 28:14-16).

The fire of God destroyed Sodom and Gomorrah, and in Jesus said that the King will say, *"Depart from Me, accursed ones, into the eternal fire which has been prepared for the devil and his angels"* (Matthew 25:41). In the last days, fire will proceed from the two witnesses and destroy their enemies (see Revelation 11:5). The fire of God destroys His enemies.

The Fire of God Is a Fire of Protection, Purging, Power, Guidance and Healing for the Believer

The Fire of God Protects Us:

> *Fire goes before Him, and burns up His adversaries round about.*   Psalm 97:3

*And of the angels He says, "Who makes His angels
winds, and His ministers a flame of fire."*
Hebrews 1:7

The morning after I was saved, I felt like I was en-
cased in a cocoon of love. Actually, it was a cocoon of
the fire of God protecting me from demon spirits, which
had previously tormented me. I sensed the presence of
demons which had been oppressing me, but now they
were outside of this cocoon and could in no way come
inside. Therefore, they could no longer oppress me.

We remember Elijah asking God to open the eyes of
his servant so he could see the chariots of fire surrounding them. The fire of God always surrounds and protects
every believer who is completely surrendered to God.

The Fire of God Purges Us:

*We went through fire and through water; yet Thou
didst bring us out into a place of abundance.*
Psalm 66:12

The fire of God purges every one of the pregnant ones
so they will not have to endure the wrath of God during
the labor pains (the Great Tribulation). Indeed in this
last hour, we will be purged, purified and refined to prepare us for the Birth (the Rapture):

I have tested you in the furnace of affliction.
Isaiah 48:10

Many pregnant ones feel that they are being tested severely in this hour, and indeed they are. God the Physician, is teaching us to trust Him as never before. He is the God of fire.

The Fire of God Gives Us Power:

This began on the Day of Pentecost, but it will continue through the birthing process. Most of the Church, even the Charismatic/Pentecostal branch, has not experienced the kind of power I am speaking of here. Remember, God created the world with the spoken word. Soon, He will demonstrate His awesome power to the Church as never before:

> *And when they had prayed, the place where they had gathered together was shaken, and they were all filled with the Holy Spirit, and began to speak the word of God with boldness.*   Acts 4:31

Have we seen this kind of power? Before the birth takes place, we will be restored to the power of the first-century Church. Because of great persecution and tribulation, the Church in some countries of the world is even now seeing power like that experienced in the Church in the first century. We hear testimonies of some of the same miracles of the book of Acts occurring in other persecuted countries. In still other places, they are hearing the Gospel of power for the first time in the history of their country. Since they have not been taught that we have lost the power, they have it! With a simple, childlike faith they walk in the same power as Peter and Paul. Oh, that we spoiled Christians can once again believe and walk in the power that will bring forth this Child!

The Physician has already given us the prescription for this power, and His desire is to restore this power in its fullness before the birth can take place. He has given us our prenatal vitamins in the form of His Word. Daily partaking of His prescription will build our faith, and thus increase His power in our lives. We will need this power in the final days before the birth. We will need this power to miraculously deliver us from prison, while the guards are asleep, and we will need this power to break the chains off of us in the middle of the night.

Remember that the Bridegroom comes to receive His Bride in the middle of the night. We will need this power to translate us to places we need to go, but cannot, in the natural. The list goes on and on. The power that was present when the Church was conceived is the same power that will be present at the birth of the Child. His fire has always been, and always will be, in the form of power.

The Fire of God Brings Guidance to the Believer:

The fire of God is especially needed during the dark night of the soul. Remember that it was the pillar of fire by night that led the children of Israel and protected them from the Egyptians. You can trust the pillar of fire. He will guide you in your darkest hour. He will bring light to your situation when it seems that the darkness of confusion is everywhere. He will guide you in the paths of righteousness. But in all this, His real purpose is to teach you to trust Him. He is the great Physician. His fire is available to guide every man who will open the door for Him.

> *Behold, I stand at the door and knock; if anyone*
> *hears My voice and opens the door, I will come in*
> *to him, and will dine with him, and he with Me.*
> Revelation 3:20

In a troubled world (that will become even more troubled as the childbirth draws near), we will need the fire of guidance continually. It may mean the difference between life and death for some of us. It is imperative that every believer fine-tune his listening skills during this gestation period. The instructions of the Physician must be heard in order for us to make it through the labor pains, and ultimately, the birth. The Physician gives us everything we need. His fire of guidance will show us the way.

The Fire of God Is a Healing Fire:

Many people, who have been healed by God, describe a sensation of heat going through their bodies. As John G. Lake prayed for people, many could feel intense heat coming through his hands into their bodies as they received their healing. Of course, John G. Lake was only a vessel who allowed the healing power of the Holy Spirit to flow through him. God has used many vessels to transport His fire of healing since the beginning of the Church. He still uses them today.

Many years ago, when we pastored our first church in northwest Florida, I was preaching my Sunday morning message. I noticed a couple visiting that I had never seen before. I was delighted, as most young pastors are, as I saw them make their way to me after the service. I immediately noticed a seriousness about them, and sensed I was in for some heavy-duty counseling. I was not prepared for what I heard.

The couple wanted me to marry them. I told them I would be happy to if they would come in for the necessary counseling I always did with couples. The woman said, "You don't understand. I'm dying of cancer, in the last stages, and only have a few weeks to live. We are living together and want to get everything right before God." I immediately shifted into another gear and told them I would marry them. After a simple ceremony the following week, I was pleased to see them in services on most Sundays.

During one service soon after that, I was bringing my morning message to an end when the young woman came to the altar and pulled me aside. "This morning," she said, "when you were preaching, I felt something leave the pulpit area, come toward me, and heat go through my body. I believe I'm healed. Do you want me to testify?" I thought for a moment, and then I told her no. I could see her dying the next week after she had testified of being healed, and that would make me look foolish. "Go to the doctor and get things checked out," I told her. "Then come back and testify." The next week she flew to California to a clinic and had a barrage of tests. There was no cancer. Needless to say, I did let her testify upon her return.

While I was preaching a revival in Georgetown, South Carolina, the fire of God was manifested in what resembled a lightning bolt as a man was totally healed of Parkinson's disease. He had been in the last stages of the disease and had gone to seventeen different specialists.

During the altar call that night, God directed me to go to the man (who was sitting on the front pew) and stand him up. He was shaking uncontrollably and could not stand without a cane. The Lord told me to hold him. As I placed my arms around him, I felt the love of God flow out of me into him. I held him for what seemed like an eternity.

Then the Lord spoke to me and told me to say to him, "Peace, be still." When I said that, he stopped shaking, and I felt my faith rise. Following the instruction of the Lord, I took his cane and threw it away. I told him to follow me and began to walk across the church.

I was almost afraid to look back, but the next thing I knew, the man had passed me by. Then he began running and jumped up on the three-foot-high stage, where he picked up an electric guitar and began to play it. That was more than a year ago, and that man is still healed and walking today. Needless to say, that miracle totally changed the service. The holy awe we felt fill the room silenced the congregation and sent us to our knees.

The healing fire of God is available for us today. The

Physician has always brought, and still does bring, the healing fire to His children.

God Always Answers His True Ministers by Fire

Each man's work will become evident; for the day will show it, because it is to be revealed with fire; and the fire itself will test the quality of each man's work.   1 Corinthians 3:13

God still answers His true ministers by fire. He does not answer by programs, sensationalism, legalism, oratory, humor, professionalism, intellect, musical talent, charm or charisma. He answers by fire. Much of the work, programs and philosophies the Church has produced will not stand the test of God's fire. God will find the quality of work to be inferior when it is inspected by the chief fire marshal, the Holy Spirit. God has always answered by fire:

And Moses and Aaron went into the tent of meeting. When they came out and blessed the people, the glory of the LORD appeared to all the people. Then fire came out from before the LORD and consumed the burnt offering and the portions of fat on the altar; and when all the people saw it, they shouted and fell on their faces. Leviticus 9:23-24

This was the first ordination service in the Bible. All the people present that day recognized that God had answered Moses and Aaron by fire. How many of our methods would we abandon today if God's outward manifestation of fire was required before the people of God recognized our leadership?

King David sinned when he decided he was proud of his large congregation. He counted them one day, only to have the number reduced by seventy thousand because of his own pride. God is not impressed with our large, backslidden, carnal churches, many of which are not churches at all, but glorified social clubs. God's dealing with David led him to repent quickly. Many preachers today need to repent of being number-conscious, rather than God-conscious:

> *Then David built an altar to the LORD there, and offered burnt offerings and peace offerings. And he called to the LORD and He answered him with fire from heaven on the altar of burnt offering.*
>
> 1 Chronicles 21:26

The Physician will answer the repentance of His true ministers with fire. His fire accepts our offering of repentance and kindles the flame within our hearts once again.

God answered many more of His true ministers by fire. He answered Elijah by fire. We may remember that Elijah challenged the false prophets of Baal to a contest. Elijah said, "We'll both call on our gods, and the one who answers by fire is the true God."

The prophets of Baal responded, "That's a good idea."

The prophets of Baal, of course, were wasting their

time calling on someone who never existed. The response was different when Elijah called on his God.

> *Answer me, O LORD, answer me, that this people*
> *may know that Thou, O LORD, art God, and that*
> *Thou hast turned their heart back again. Then the*
> *fire of the LORD fell, and consumed the burnt offer-*
> *ing and the wood and the stones and the dust, and*
> *licked up the water that was in the trench. And*
> *when all the people saw it, they fell on their faces;*
> *and they said, "The LORD, He is God; the LORD, He*
> *is God.*   1 Kings 18:37-39

God answered Elijah by fire, and this fire was the sign that God's anointing was on the prophet. What would happen if this was our means of measuring the anointing of God on His ministers today? Many would have to start looking for other professions.

God answered Solomon by fire at the dedication of the Temple (see 2 Chronicles 7:1-2). The glory of the Lord filled the Temple, and the priests could not stand to minister. There have been times when I could no longer stand because of the power of God in a service. I could no longer preach. Those were the best services I have ever experienced. But that is just the tip of the iceberg. God's glory is about to come to His house in a dimension that will astound even the greatest prophets among us.

We must be careful to approach the fire of God with caution and humility. We must also be careful not to warm ourselves by the wrong fire, like Peter did after he betrayed Jesus. He found himself being warmed by the fire of worldly comfort. Jesus had gone to the cross, and Peter did not want to follow. You can never have the Pentecostal power until you have been through the crucifying, purging fire of God. Many so-called Spirit-filled Christians today are experiencing the fire of worldly comfort like Peter, rather than the true fire of God, which means death to self. How would we evaluate our ministries today if we knew the fire of God was our measuring tool? Much of our ministries would be burned up by the fire of God. God always has, and always will, answer His true ministers by fire.

We Return the Fire of God Back to Him in Worship:

Its entrails however, and its legs he shall wash with water. And the priest shall offer up in smoke all of it on the altar for a burnt offering, an offering by fire of a soothing aroma to the LORD.

Leviticus 1:9

Then he shall tear it by its wings, but shall not sever it. And the priest shall offer it up in smoke on the altar on the wood which is on the fire; it is a burnt offering, AN OFFERING BY FIRE OF A SOOTHING AROMA TO THE LORD. Leviticus 1:17

Then Aaron's sons shall offer it up in smoke on the altar on the burnt offering, which is on the wood that is on the fire; it is AN OFFERING BY FIRE OF A SOOTHING AROMA TO THE LORD.

Leviticus 3:5

And the priest shall offer them up in smoke on the altar as food, AN OFFERING BY FIRE FOR A SOOTHING AROMA; all fat is the LORD's.
Leviticus 3:16

In the Old Testament, when animal sacrifices were made, the animal was consumed by fire, the essence of the animal being reduced to vapor. When a man sacrificed an animal in his stead, his innermost being (his heart) ascended to God in vapor. To have true worship, the worship that returns the fire of God back to Him, there must be an offering by fire for a soothing aroma to the Lord. The worship must come from the innermost being of the worshipper. David said, *"Behold thou dost desire truth in the innermost being, and in the hidden part thou wilt make me to know wisdom"* (Psalm 51:6). True worship from the pregnant ones will cause their flesh to be very uncomfortable. The flesh must be put to death so that the spirit can worship.

But thanks be to God, who always leads us in His triumph in Christ, and manifests through us the sweet aroma of the knowledge of Him in every place. For we are a fragrance of Christ to God among those who are being saved and among those who are perishing; to the one an aroma from death to death, to the other an aroma from life to life.
2 Corinthians 2:14-16

If we are to be a sweet-smelling fragrance of Christ to God, our flesh must be put to death. It must burn up.

The fat belongs to the Lord. And — spiritually speaking — how much fat there is! Much of what we consider worship is really no more than our spirits enjoying the presence of God. There is nothing wrong with this, but we must not confuse this with offering the fire of God back to Him. The greatest act of worship that has ever been was the freewill offering of the perfect sacrifice of our Lord as He willingly, in obedience, endured the cross as a sacrifice for our sins.

Let me ask you a question. Do you think this was a comfortable experience for His flesh? Do you think it was comfortable for Paul and Silas, after being beaten half to death, to lift up praises to God in prison? Do you think it was comfortable for John the Baptist to praise God from prison, just prior to being decapitated? Do you think it was comfortable for the flesh of Peter to be crucified upside down? Do you think it was comfortable for John on the Isle of Patmos? For Daniel in exile? For Jeremiah in the well? For David in the cave? For Gideon in captivity? The list goes on and on. Think about it, and I'm sure you will come to the conclusion that the greatest acts of worship you have given to God were not comfortable to your flesh.

It is easy to worship God when things are going well, but what about when you don't feel like it — when you are in the midst of a battle, when your world seems to be caving in? Worship during these times is a true, sweet-smelling aroma to God. The sacrifice of dying to self, to your flesh and to what others think about you, is a sweet-smelling aroma to God.

Earlier in the book, I shared my testimony about receiving the baptism of the Holy Spirit the night after I was saved. I truly believe the fire of God came upon me that night because of my obedience in standing in a public restaurant and confessing Jesus as Lord the night before. To the degree that our flesh hurts, to that same degree our true worship is offered up to God.

We have all smelled bacon cooking. What a wonderful smell first thing in the morning! In the same way, the burning up of our flesh smells like bacon to God. He likes it.

In the Old Testament, the fire was kept burning continually upon the altar. Our fire of worship to God must be continually climbing upward if we are to live a victorious life. This is pleasing to Him. All day long we can be in an attitude of communion, praise, prayer and worship unto Him. This is what the Physician desires from us.

> *Fire shall be kept burning continually on the altar;*
> *it is not to go out.*   Leviticus 6:13

As the ninth month approaches and the birth is near, multitudes of believers will catch this revelation of continual praise and worship. They will find that this is one of the main keys in keeping their faith level high for the labor pains. Mike Bickle recently started the International House of Prayer, a twenty-four-a-day prayer ministry. He resigned from Metro Christian Fellowship, his three thousand member church congregation in Kansas City, Missouri. He believes twenty-four-hour-a-day meetings, combining intense worship and prophetic prayer, will change the spiritual atmosphere of cities.

Our offering by fire of worship to God is really feeding God:

> *For every beast of the forest is Mine, the cattle on a thousand hills. I know every bird of the mountains, and everything that moves in the field is Mine. If I were hungry, I would not tell you; for the world is Mine, and all it contains. Shall I eat the flesh of bulls, or drink the blood of male goats? Offer to God a sacrifice of thanksgiving, and pay your vows to the Most High; and call upon Me in the day of trouble; I shall rescue you, and you will honor Me.*
> Psalm 50:10-15

As the pregnant ones sacrificially offer their worship unto God, and trust God the Physician, this Child within will be birthed. There is no problem that He doesn't already have the prescription for. The Physician (God the Father) will meet every need of the pregnant ones. He desires us to be whole and healthy for the upcoming birth.

Endnote

1. *The Seven Festivals of the Messiah*, Edward Chumney, Destiny Image Publishers, Inc., Shippensburg, PA, 1994, p. 81.

Chapter 8

The Husband

For I am jealous for you with a godly jealousy; for I betrothed you to one husband, that to Christ I might present you as a pure virgin.

2 Corinthians 11:2

For your husband is your Maker, whose name is the LORD *of hosts; and your Redeemer is the Holy One of Israel, who is called the God of all the earth.*

Isaiah 54:5

A man's contribution is vital to the birth of his baby. Without him the picture is not complete. His wife could face the birth without him, but it would be contrary to God's plan for the human race. The husband is at his wife's side from the beginning to the end (from the conception to the birth), and in our case, the Husband is Jesus.

Jesus is always interceding for His Bride, the Church. He chose this Bride before the foundation of the world. It was His preordained plan that His seed of promise should be carried by His Old Testament covenant people until the appointed time of the conception. From that time on, He has been at the right hand of the Father interceding for His Bride.

> *Hence, also, He is able to save forever those who draw near to God through Him, since HE ALWAYS LIVES TO MAKE INTERCESSION FOR THEM.* Hebrews 7:25

Now, the Husband is on His way to the hospital, where the Physician will deliver this baby in perfect health. How excited and expectant He is! Truly, He is soon to rejoice over His people with great joy.

It has not always been this way. There were many dark hours when it seemed that there would be a miscarriage. Had it not been for the faithfulness and prayers of the Husband, the Bride would not have made it this far, because the abortionist was always standing just outside the door with his evil scalpel in his hand. He was able to kill many of God's chosen vessels, but he could not destroy this Child, because of the faithfulness of the Husband.

The Husband has been praying for His Bride so that she might become the radiance of His glory and the exact representation of His nature, even as He is the radiance of His Father's glory and the exact representation of His Father's nature (see Hebrews 1:3).

The Husband has always been Emmanuel to the Bride. He has always been with her. He was with her at conception on the Day of Pentecost. It was He who sent the Teacher to her that day. The Teacher appeared in great power and wisdom, so that the Bride would never doubt His ability.

Luke records the conception and the first month of the pregnancy in the book of Acts. There, we see the Husband interceding for the Bride as she becomes very healthy — in spite of continued harassment from the abortionist:

The first account I composed, Theophilus, about all that Jesus began to do and teach, until the day when He was taken up, after He had by the Holy Spirit given orders to the apostles whom He had chosen. To these He also presented Himself alive, after His suffering, by many convincing proofs, appearing to them over a period of forty days, and speaking of the things concerning the kingdom of God. And gathering them together, He commanded them not to leave Jerusalem, but to wait for what the Father had promised, "Which," He said, "you heard of from Me; for John baptized with water, but you shall be baptized with the Holy Spirit not many days from now."   Acts 1:1-5

And when the day of Pentecost had come, they were all together in one place. And suddenly there came from heaven a noise like a violent, rushing wind, and it filled the whole house where they were sitting. And there appeared to them tongues as of fire distributing themselves, and they rested on each one of them. And they were all filled with the Holy Spirit and began to speak with other tongues, as the Spirit was giving them utterance.   Acts 2:1-4

It was the Husband who was at the right hand of His

Father interceding for the Bride. It was the Husband who appeared to Paul on the Damascus road and gave him the great revelation that would strengthen the Bride in centuries to come. It was the Husband who instructed Peter that the Gentiles were also heirs of this Kingdom by faith. It was the Husband who sent out His disciples throughout the world to spread the great news that the Bride was pregnant and would soon give birth. Luke recorded all of these events and many more, but the book of Acts is still in the process of being written, and the Husband is still to be found always at the side of His Bride.

The human race was created in the image and likeness of God for one purpose: to provide an eternal companion for the Son. After the fall and the promise of redemption through the coming Messiah, the Messianic race (Israel) was born and nurtured in order to bring the Messiah into the world. The Messiah came for one intent, and only one — to give birth to His Church, and thus, to obtain His Bride. The Church then — the called-out body of redeemed mankind — turns out to be the central object, the goal, not only of mundane history but also of all that God has been doing in all realms, from all eternity.

The Husband's Role Throughout the History of the Church

The Early Months of Pregnancy:

The Husband was interceding for the Bride at the fall of Jerusalem in AD 70. According to the historian

Josephus, He warned the Christians to flee Jerusalem, and they did and were spared the horrors that Vespasian, the Roman general, inflicted upon all those living in that city. The Husband was with His Bride when many of the saints were persecuted under the rule of the emperor Domitian. Even though there was great persecution during the first years of the Church's existence (the first months of pregnancy), the Child within grew stronger and healthier.

Since persecution did not work to discourage the believers, the abortionist had another plan that would have succeeded had it not been for the faithful Husband standing beside His Bride. When Constantine made Christianity the state religion, he opened the way for the beginning of the Dark Ages. It was not until the faithful intercession of the Husband raised up the reformer Martin Luther that light and health began to come into the Church once again. Some believe this thousand-year period of the Dark Ages was the great apostasy, and I concur. In my opinion, Dr. Bill Hamon has written the best account of Church history through the eyes of the Holy Spirit in his book *The Eternal Church.*

The Fifth Month of Pregnancy:

The Husband then raised up another prophet, John Wycliffe (1329-1384), to further strengthen His Bride. Wycliffe translated the Bible from the Vulgate into English. This further strengthened the Bride and her Child within. At this time, she was approximately in the fifth month of pregnancy.

Then the Husband raised up the prophet John Huss (1369-1415). He taught that only Christ could forgive sins. He was condemned and burned at the stake, but not before the Husband had used him greatly.

The Sixth Month of Pregnancy:

In the sixth month of pregnancy, the child within began to grow more rapidly. The Bride needed more nutrition and the Husband interceded with the Father until the printing press was invented in 1456. This made the Word of God available to the common man, which later sparked the Reformation.

Late in the sixth month of pregnancy, the Husband raised up His chosen vessel, Martin Luther, to further bruise the abortionist by experiencing and preaching the doctrine of justification by faith. Of this, Dr. Bill Hamon wrote: "Luther was a man God used to lead the Church out of its religious Egyptian bondage fifteen hundred years after the coming of Christ, as Moses was the man who led the children of Israel out of their literal Egyptian bondage fifteen hundred years before the coming of the Messiah. Other men in other countries arose to propagate the same truth: Ulrich Zwingli, John Calvin, John Tyndale, John Knox, Philip Melanchthon, Martin Bucher. These are the men best known for their contributions to the great Protestant Movement." [2]

As this doctrine strengthened the Babe, the Bride could now feel the kicks from within. Further stretch marks appeared upon the Bride as the preaching of John Calvin,

John Tyndale, John Knox and Philip Melanchthon nourished the Child. However, these stretch marks brought pain to the Bride, as the number of martyrs resulting from persecution by religious leaders of the day outnumbered the early Christian martyrs under pagan Rome.

The Seventh Month of Pregnancy:

In the seventh month of pregnancy, the Husband continued to intercede until the doctrine of sanctification was restored to the Church. The resulting movement came to be called the Holiness Movement. John Wesley was the primary preacher to receive the revelation of sanctification from the Husband. Others, like Jonathan Edwards, George Whitefield, Charles Finney and William Booth, were also raised up in this period to further nourish the Child within.

The Eighth Month of Pregnancy:

In the eighth month, through the intercession of the Husband, the doctrine of the baptism of the Holy Spirit was restored through the Pentecostal Movement at the turn of the twentieth century. What a joy for the Husband, for the Bride and for the Child within on that day as power was restored to the Church. The Husband continued to intercede for the Bride as the doctrine of divine healing was restored in the Latter Rain Movement, and then the gifts of the Holy Spirit were restored in the Charismatic Movement.

The Ninth Month of Pregnancy:

The Husband is presently interceding for His Bride, for the time of her delivery is drawing near:

> *Repent therefore and return, that your sins may be wiped away, in order that times of refreshing may come from the presence of the Lord; and that He may send Jesus, the Christ appointed for you, whom Heaven must receive until the period of restoration of all things about which God spoke by the mouth of His holy prophets from ancient time.*   Acts 3:19-21

The Bible teaches us clearly that Jesus will be kept in Heaven until the period of restoration of all things. Even though we are in the ninth month of pregnancy, the child will not be born until all things are restored to the Church. The Husband is now interceding to the Father that the apostles and prophets be restored in the Church. As this takes place, the saints of God will begin to walk in the maturity spoken of in the New Testament epistles.

We seem so far away from this goal, and yet we are so close. In the same way, God sometimes seems so far away, and yet He is always close.

The faithfulness of the Husband guarantees us that this child will be birthed in perfect health. All authority has been given to the Husband, and He has given this authority to His Bride (the Church).

The Uniqueness of the Husband:

The Husband is like no other husband who has ever lived or ever will live. He loves His Bride and cherishes her with a love that is incomprehensible to the human mind. The Bride, in turn, loves this Husband because of the love that He has imparted to her. The Song of Solomon best describes this love:

> *May he kiss me with the kisses of his mouth! For your love is better than wine. Your oils have a pleasing fragrance, your name is like purified oil; therefore the maidens love you. Draw me after you, and let us run together! The king has brought me into his chambers.*   Song of Solomon 1:2-4

> *How beautiful you are, my darling, how beautiful you are! Your eyes are like doves. How handsome you are, my beloved, and so pleasant! Indeed, our couch is luxuriant!*   Song of Solomon 1:15-16

> *He has brought me to his banquet hall, and his banner over me is love.*   Song of Solomon 2:4

In this ninth month of pregnancy, the Bride will begin to express her love for the Husband without inhibitions, without shame, without concern for respectability, without religious or traditional restraint. The Bride will be enthralled with her Husband as the birth nears. She will have a great longing for Him. She will express her love for Him even more gracefully than the Shulammite expressed hers for Solomon.

The world will look in wonder at these love-sick pregnant ones. Demons will tremble and be dismayed, because as they see this love in full bloom, they know that their demise is near.

In this ninth month, the Husband will also express the greatness of His love for His Bride:

> *How beautiful you are, my darling, how beautiful you are! Your eyes are like doves behind your veil; your hair is like a flock of goats that have descended from Mount Gilead. Your teeth are like a flock of newly shorn ewes which have come up from their washing, all of which bear twins, and not one among them has lost her young. Your lips are like a scarlet thread, and your mouth is lovely. Your temples are like a slice of a pomegranate behind your veil.*   Song of Solomon 4:1-3

These expressions of love from the Bride to her Husband and from the Husband to His Bride cannot compare to the love the true Bride will soon experience at the birth of the Child. There is no breadth, length, height or depth to this love. It truly surpasses knowledge. Such is the love the Husband has for His Bride.

The Husband has already laid down his life for the Bride so the Bride could be released from the Law. He knew the Bride could never mature by the Law. She could only live by the Spirit:

> *For the married woman is bound by law to her husband while he is living; but if her husband dies, she*

is released from the law concerning the husband.
So then if, while her husband is living, she is joined
to another man, she shall be called an adulteress;
but if her husband dies, she is free from the law, so
that she is not an adulteress, though she is joined
to another man. Therefore, my brethren, you also
were made to die to the Law through the body of
Christ, that you might be joined to another, to Him
who was raised from the dead, that we might bear
fruit for God. For while we were in the flesh, the
sinful passions, which were aroused by the Law,
were at work in the members of our body to bear
fruit for death.   Romans 7:2-5

The Husband knew that His Bride was a violator of
the Law, and for this reason He laid down His life so
she could be free from the Law. He knew that she was
filled with all imaginable filth and sin — even before He
married her — and yet He gave all for her:

But God demonstrates His own love toward us, in
that while we were yet sinners, Christ died for us.
                                                   Romans 5:8

Only one Husband has completely loved His Bride as
God intended, but God has instructed earthly husbands
to strive for the love the true Husband has for His Bride:

Husbands, love your wives, just as Christ also loved
the church and gave Himself up for her; that He
might sanctify her, having cleansed her by the wash-

> *ing of water with the word, that He might present*
> *to Himself the church in all her glory, having no*
> *spot or wrinkle or any such thing; but that she*
> *should be holy and blameless. So husbands ought*
> *also to love their own wives as their own bodies.*
> *He who loves his own wife loves himself; for no one*
> *ever hated his own flesh, but nourishes and cher-*
> *ishes it, just as Christ also does the church, because*
> *we are members of His body. For this cause a man*
> *shall leave his father and mother, and shall cleave*
> *to his wife; and the two shall become one flesh. This*
> *mystery is great; but I am speaking with reference*
> *to Christ and the church.*   Ephesians 5:25-32

The Husband has always loved His Bride with a faithful and unfathomable love. It is the Bride (like Gomer, the bride of Hosea) who has been unfaithful and has not returned the agape love to the One who has so loved her. But this too is changing, as the lovesick pregnant ones break up their fallow ground, lay aside their garments of heaviness, put on their wedding garments and prepare to meet their kingly, magnificent Husband in the air.

Endnotes

1. *Destined for the Throne,* Paul E. Bilheimer, Christian Literature Crusade, Fort Washington, PA, 1975, p. 22.
2. *The Eternal Church,* Dr. Bill Hamon, Christian International Publishers, Phoenix, AZ, 1981, pp. 154, 155.

Chapter 9

The Birth

"Shall I bring to the point of birth, and not give delivery?" says the LORD. "Or shall I who gives delivery shut the womb?" says your God.   Isaiah 66:9

It is time for the birth. Everything the woman has anticipated during the long period of pregnancy is about to be realized. All the preparation, education and longing is about to come into play with the birth of the awaited one. As she looks to her husband and the physician for instruction and partnership, she is about to embark on the most important part of her journey. As she approaches the birth, the labor pains begin to rise and subside, becoming closer together and stronger in intensity.

All creation has longed for this moment. The Creator will now marry His chosen creation, the Church. The conception took place two thousand years ago at Pentecost. The abortionist has been notably unsuccessful in his attempts to destroy the Child. Indeed, with every attempt the Child has only become stronger.

The world has had ample opportunity to recognize that the Bride is very pregnant. Sons of God are now walking the earth in the fullness of the power and love for which they were created.

The careful reader would note that the Bride is pregnant before the marriage. We recall the first very special pregnancy. The Virgin Mary was also pregnant with Christ before her marriage to Joseph. In the same way, we are pregnant with Christ before our betrothal and marriage.

The Teacher (the Holy Spirit) is present, having completely instructed the Bride in the childbirth classes. The Bride is no longer fearful because of her lack of readiness. Perfect love has cast out all fear. The Bride has now been perfected in love. She is prepared and ready! The labor pains have now maximized. The process has been a long time in coming and not without danger of miscarriage, but now the moment has arrived. All that remains is the shout of joy.

The Husband (Jesus) is present at the Bride's side, to see the Child that He has longed for. He has always been with her, even in her darkest hours. He never once stopped praying for her. The joy that He is now experiencing He has longed for before the foundation of the world. He is ready for the honeymoon of seven years, before He and the Bride return to earth to rule and reign.

The Physician (God the Father) has watched over and protected the Bride and the Child within. He, too, is experiencing great joy as the time arrives for Him to sever the umbilical cord.

Friends and family (the angels and departed saints) share this joyful occasion. The one person who is noticeably absent is the abortionist (Satan). The time of the birth has been hidden from him, for he is a defeated foe.

The Bride is present. She has waited all these many months and longs for her marriage.

There has been, and will continue to be, an explosion of books, articles, radio and television broadcasts, sermons, movies, etc., preparing the Church for this birth. Every Christian bookstore I visit has end-time prophecy books on the front display. I cannot listen to Christian television or radio without hearing a message concerning the return of our Lord. Never before have so many movies been made concerning the end times and the Rapture of the Church. All of these means of communication will continue to multiply exponentially, announcing the birth. After all, this is the greatest event so far in the history of the Church and the world. Even as the wise men knew the birth of Christ was near, we know the second birth (the Rapture) is very near.

There may be minor differences of opinion of when this birth will occur: pre-, mid- or post-Tribulation, but all are beginning to agree that the time is very near, the Lord is knocking at the door:

> *And behold, there was a man in Jerusalem whose name was Simeon; and this man was righteous and devout, looking for the consolation of Israel; and the Holy Spirit was upon him. And it had been revealed to him by the Holy Spirit that he would not see death before he had seen the Lord's Christ. And he came in the Spirit into the temple; and when the parents brought in the child Jesus, to carry out for Him the custom of the Law, then he took Him into*

*his arms, and blessed God, and said, "Now Lord,
Thou dost let Thy bond-servant depart in peace,
according to Thy word; for my eyes have seen Thy
salvation, which Thou hast prepared in the presence of all peoples, a light of revelation to the
Gentiles, and the glory of Thy people Israel."*

Luke 2:25-32

Even as Simeon knew that he would not die before
the Christ's appearing, it will be revealed by the Holy
Spirit to many that they will not die before the Birth (the
Rapture).

Edward Chumney sees the Rapture coming on Rosh
Hashanah in the season of Teshuvah in his book *The
Seven Festivals of the Messiah*: "Thirty days into Teshuvah
comes Rosh Hashanah and ending on the fortieth day
with Yom Kippur. The shofar is blown after every morning service for thirty days. Psalm 89:15 says, *'How blessed
are the people who know the joyful sound [blast of the sho-
far].'* The commandment is to hear the sound of the
shofar. A theme associated with Rosh Hashanah is *to
awake*. Another name for Rosh Hashanah is Yom HaDin,
the Day of Judgment.

"It has been taught that the school of Shammai says
that there will be three classes on the final Day of Judgment, one for the holy righteous, one for the holy wicked,
and one for the intermediates. The righteous are separated and will be with God. This is known to Bible
believers as the Rapture, which in Hebrew is the Natzal.
The wicked will face the wrath of God during the Tribulation period, and will never repent. The average person

has until Yom Kippur until his fate is sealed forever. In other words, the average person will have until the end of the seven-year Tribulation to repent and to turn to God." [1]

Dr. Bill Hamon describes this Birth (the Rapture) in his book *Apostles, Prophets, and the Coming Moves of God:* "None of God's saints have gotten out of this world alive in their physical bodies. All have been taken out by the agent of death. Satan is determined that none will ever leave without dying, but Jesus has other plans (1 Cor. 15:51-54; 2 Cor. 5:4; 1 Thess. 4:13 -18; 2 Thess. 1:5 - 11; Ps. 102:18-20; Rom. 8:23).

"Somewhere between the Army of the Lord Movement and close to the end of the Kingdom-Establishing Movement, Jesus will arise from the seat of the right hand of the Father. He will leap forth with His sword in His hand and give a shout that rings out to the ends of the universe and all over planet earth. He will shout, 'Devil, you have had it, and the angel of death, your power over My Church is canceled and destroyed.' He will have His archangels sounding the trumpet of the Lord as He shouts to His Church: 'Delay shall not be one minute longer, for it is time for your final redemption and victory over death.'

"As He is shouting this, He is descending from Heaven faster than the speed of light. He brings with Him all the saints who have lost their bodies to death. As He comes into earth's atmosphere, He shouts again, and in a moment, in the twinkling of an eye, all the bodies of the saints ascend to meet the Lord and be joined with their spirit beings. These bodies become eternally indestructible and never see death again." [2]

Finnis Jennings Dake describes the birth as follows: "The Rapture of the Church is called the 'Coming of the Lord' but never the Second Coming of Christ. At the Rapture, Christ does not appear visibly to those on the earth, but He comes in the air above the earth to catch up, or rapture, the dead and living saints who rise together to meet the Lord in the air. The Rapture is purely a New Testament doctrine and was first revealed to Paul as a special revelation (1 Corinthians 15:51-58), while the second coming of Christ is not only a New Testament doctrine, but is one of the chief themes of the Old Testament. The Old Testament prophets never saw the New Testament Church, much less the Rapture of the Church.

"The purpose of the Rapture is to resurrect the just from the dead and take all the saints out of the world before the Tribulation comes, in order that they may have fulfilled in them the purpose for which God has saved them." [3]

Adam Clarke describes the Rapture as follows: "The Lord himself, that is: Jesus Christ shall descend from heaven; shall descend in like manner as he was seen by his disciples to ascend, i.e. in his human form, but now infinitely more glorious; for thousands of thousands shall minister unto him, and ten thousand times ten thousand shall stand before him; for the Son of man shall come on the throne of his glory: but who may abide the day of his coming, or stand when he appeareth? The eternal states of quick and dead being thus determined, then all who shall be found to have made a covenant with him by sacrifice, and to have washed their robes, and made them white in the blood of the Lamb, shall be taken to his eternal glory, and be forever with the Lord. What an inexpressibly terrific glory will then be exhibited! I forbear to call in here the descriptions which men of a poetic turn have made of this terrible scene, because I cannot trust to their correctness; and it is a subject which we should speak of and contemplate as nearly as possible in the words of Scripture." [4]

There are several types and shadows of the Rapture in the Old Testament. Enoch is the first. He was a godly man, a set-apart man, a holy man, a man after God's own heart. He was like one of the pregnant ones. He drew closer and closer to God, until God removed him from the earth:

> *And Enoch walked with God; and he was not, for*
> *God took him.*   Genesis 5:24

Elijah also was a type of the pregnant ones. God was well pleased with him. As Elijah was walking along with his servant one day, having completed his earthly ministry, God brought him to Heaven in a whirlwind:

> *Then it came about as they were going along and*
> *talking, that behold, there appeared a chariot of fire*
> *and horses of fire which separated the two of them.*
> *And Elijah went up by a whirlwind to heaven.*
>   2 Kings 2:11

The Lord Jesus Himself ascended into Heaven as a forerunner for us, a type of things to come. After His death, burial and resurrection, He gave orders by the

Holy Spirit to the apostles. He remained on earth for forty days and taught them many things. Then it came time for His departure:

> *And after He had said these things, He was lifted up while they were looking on, and a cloud received Him out of their sight. And as they were gazing intently into the sky while He was departing, behold, two men in white clothing stood beside them; and they also said, "Men of Galilee, why do you stand looking into the sky? This Jesus, who has been taken up from you into heaven, will come in just the same way as you have watched Him go into heaven."*   Acts 1:9-11

Jesus spoke of His return to earth in comforting words in the gospel of John:

> *Let not your heart be troubled; believe in God, believe also in Me. In My Father's house are many dwelling places; if it were not so, I would have told you; for I go to prepare a place for you. And if I go and prepare a place for you, I will come again, and receive you to Myself; that where I am, there you may be also.*   John 14:1-3

Paul spoke of the Rapture as follows:

> *For the Lord Himself will descend from heaven with a shout, with the voice of the archangel, and with the trumpet of God; and the dead in Christ shall*

*rise first. Then we who are alive and remain shall
be caught up together with them in the clouds to
meet the Lord in the air, and thus we shall always
be with the Lord.*   1 Thessalonians 4:16-17

*Behold, I tell you a mystery; we shall not all sleep,
but we shall all be changed, in a moment, in the
twinkling of an eye, at the last trumpet; for the
trumpet will sound, and the dead will be raised
imperishable, and we shall be changed.*
                                    1 Corinthians 15:51-52

What a day that will be! The pregnant ones have endured the afflictions and tribulations in the world and
have been *overcomers*. They have been tempted in every
way possible by the abortionist, yet they have been *overcomers*. They have been treated as outcasts in a world
which is not their home, and they have been *overcomers*.
From the time of the conception of the Christ Child, they
have walked in a manner worthy of the Lord, to please
Him in all respects. When they stumbled in their walk,
they simply asked Him to forgive them, and He washed
away their sins with His blood. Thus, they were *overcomers*. They walked through the period of recognition,
which brought great reproach upon them, because they
no longer resembled the world in any way. Again, they
were *overcomers*, considering the reproach of Christ and
the sufferings of Christ as not worthy to be compared
with the glory that will be revealed to them.

They completed the difficult childbirth classes taught
by the Holy Spirit and endured the long hours of study

as *overcomers*. They endured the uncomfortable labor pains as *overcomers*. They learned to trust the Physician and became *overcomers*. The Husband prayed for them until they emerged as *overcomers*.

Finally, it is time! All creation is expectantly awaiting this birth. God the Father takes the scalpel and cuts the umbilical cord. The Child is birthed. The Bride meets the Husband in the air. Now the nine-month gestation period is a dull memory. All tears have been wiped away from all eyes. Now there is no more death, no more groaning, no more sorrow and no more pain.

The time is very near, even at the door, but until it comes, we remain *Pregnant With Christ.*

Endnotes

1. *The Seven Festivals of the Messiah,* Edward Chumney, Destiny Image Publishers, Inc., Shippensburg, PA, 1994, pp. 95, 99, 105.
2. *Apostles, Prophets and the Coming Moves of God,* Dr. Bill Hamon, Destiny Image Publishers. Inc., Shippensburg, PA, 1997, pp. 263, 264.
3. *God's Plan for Man,* Finnis Jennings Dake, Dake Bible Sales, Inc., Lawrenceville, GA, 1946, p. 840.
4. *Adam Clarke's Commentary,* Adam Clark, Electronic Database, copyright © 1996 by Biblesoft.

Epilogue

Have you been impregnated by God's Spirit?

Perhaps, in reading this book, you have realized, through the conviction of the Holy Spirit, that you are not *Pregnant With Christ*. You don't want to find yourself in this end time without conception. My friend, the solution is very simple. Please consider praying the following prayer:

Lord Jesus,

Please come into my heart and save me. Wash away all my sins with Your blood, and give me the gift of eternal life.

Amen!

Bibliography

Allen, A.A., *God's Guarantee to Heal You*, Schambach Revivals, Inc., Tyler, Texas, 1991.

Annacondia, Carlos, *Listen to Me, Satan*, Creation House, Lake Mary, Florida, 1998.

Bartleman, Frank, *Azusa Street*, Whitaker House, New Kensington, Pennsylvania, 1982.

Billheimer, Paul E., *Destined for the Throne*, Christian Literature Crusade, Fort Washington, Pennsylvania, 1965.

Cho, Dr. David Yonggi, *Prayer That Brings Revival*, Creation House, Lake Mary, Florida, 1998.

Chumney, Edward, *The Seven Festivals of the Messiah*, Destiny Image Publishers, Inc., Shippensburg, Pennsylvania, 1994.

Clark, Adam, *Adam Clarke's Commentary*, Electronic Database, copyright © 1996 by Biblesoft.

Dake, Finnis Jennings, *God's Plan for Man*, Dake Bible Sales, Inc., Lawrenceville, GA, 1946.

Hagin, Kenneth E., *The New Birth*, Rhema Bible Church, Kenneth Hagin Ministries, Inc., 1975.

Hamon, Dr. Bill, *Apostles, Prophets and the Coming Moves of God*, Destiny Image Publishers, Inc., Shippensburg, Pennsylvania, 1997.

Hamon, Dr. Bill, *The Eternal Church*, Christian International Publishing, Phoenix, Arizona, 1981.

Hurnard, Hannah, *Hinds' Feet on High Places*, Living Books, Tyndale House Publishers, Wheaton, Illinois, 1977.

Hywel-Davies, Jack, *The Life of Smith Wigglesworth*, Vine Books, Servant Publications, Ann Arbor, Michigan, 1987, by Hodder and Stoughton Limited, First American Edition 1988 by Servant Books.

Johnson, Nita, *Prepare for the Winds of Change II*, Eagle's Nest Publishing, Clovis, California, 1991.

Joyner, Rick, *Overcoming the Accuser*, Morningstar Publications, Charlotte, North Carolina, 1996.

Joyner, Rick, *The Final Quest*, Whitaker House, New Kensington, Pennsylvania, 1996.

Joyner, Rick, *The Fire That Could Not Die,* Morningstar Publications, Charlotte, North Carolina, 1998.

Lawrence, Brother, *The Practice of the Presence of God*, CBN University Press, Virginia Beach, Virginia, 1978.

Lewis, C.S., *The Screwtape Letters*, Lord and King Associates, Inc., West Chicago, Illinois, 1976.

Liardon, Roberts, *God's Generals*, Albury Publishing, Tulsa, Oklahoma, 1996.

Liardon, Roberts, *John G. Lake: The Complete Collection of His Life Teachings*, Albury Publishing, Tulsa, Oklahoma, 1999.

McDaniel, Burt, *Seize the Day,* Morris Publishing, Kearney, Nebraska, 1996.

Murray, Andrew, *Abide in Christ,* Marshall, Morgan & Scott, Ltd., London, 1968, Christian Literature Crusade, Ft. Washington, Pennsylvania, 1974.

The Holy Bible, New American Standard Version, The Lockman Foundation, LaHabra, California, 1960, 1962, 1963, 1968, 1971, 1972, 1973, 1975, 1977.

The Holy Bible, New International Version, International Bible Society, Colorado Springs, CO, 1973, 1978, 1984.

Schmitt, Charles P., *Floods Upon the Dry Ground,* Destiny Image Publishers, Shippensburg, Pennsylvania, 1998.

Tozer, A.W., *The Pursuit of God,* Christian Publications, Camp Hill, Pennsylvania, 1982, 1993.

Wilkerson, David, *America's Last Call*, Wilkerson Trust Publications, Lindale, Texas, 1998.

The Carters are available for ministy. You may contact them at the following address:

Phillip and Vivian Carter
SONrise Evangelistic Association, Inc.
P.O. Box 2863
Alpharetta, GA 30023-2863
770-418-1134
CartersSonrise@cs.com